THE
JUNGLE
SCHOOL

The
JUNGLE
School

Written in Indonesian by
Butet Manurung

Jakarta, Indonesia

Translated by Anya Robertson and Tiro A. Daenuwy
Edited by Gouri Mirpuri and Ro King

Yayasan Sokola, Jenggala 1 no. 7, Depnakertrans-Kranji Bekasi, Indonesia 17145

Design & Layout: Sokola Design Team
Photos: Sokola Team
Cover: Cindy Saja

First Edition published in Indonesian as *Sokola Rimba* by INSIST Press, 2007

www.sokola.org

This book was printed in the United States of America.

To order additional copies of this book, contact:
Xlibris Corporation
1-888-795-4274
www.Xlibris.com
Orders@Xlibris.com
111907

Contents

Praise for *The Jungle School*

"The traditional wisdom of the indigenous people of Indonesia is a truth that we must preserve. At the same time, the dilemma between introducing modernity, development and education while protecting their traditional way of life is another truth. I greatly appreciate the contribution and dedication of people like Butet Manurung who provide true insights into the Orang Rimba. *The Jungle School* speaks volumes from actual experience, recorded not only in an anthropological way, but also in a very human and personal way. This is a book that not only makes us realize that traditional wisdom and jungles need to be preserved, but also warms the heart."

Mari Pangestu, Indonesia's Minister of Tourism and Creative Economy

"The Jungle School puts a human face on the results of logging and deforestation practices that directly threaten the existence of the Orang Rimba. Although the rights of the often-forgotten Rimba people are protected by our laws, their aspirations are sometimes ignored in the management of rainforests and their resources. Education for the Rimba is truly a gift for life. Butet's story will change the hearts and minds of those who think otherwise."

Agus Purnomo, Special Staff to the President of the Republic of Indonesia for Climate Change

"The challenges for educators are endless. Yet, instead of cursing the darkness, Butet Manurung has chosen to give light. She combines her love of nature with her passion for children and education. In *The Jungle School*, she shows us that great schools do not depend on grand buildings or high-tech systems. The soul of education rests with each teacher. It is the teacher who stands in front of the class—to educate and inspire the children and to be their role model.

Our options are simple: curse the darkness or give light. Butet shines her light in the depths of the jungles of Indonesia and I am sure that light will continue to brighten our society. This is a book of inspiration!"

Anies Baswedan, Rector, Paramadina University

"*The Jungle School* comes at a critical moment in the development of the present civilization. It combats all the theoretical complexity of educational developments to smooth the process from literate society to knowledge society; welfare society to cultured and civilized society.

Butet Manurung shows that the impossible is possible by touching the hearts and minds of the Orang Rimba, by reaching the unreachable soul of an indigenous community, by helping us to understand what it means to be human. She inspires readers and takes them on a journey of educational adventure that highlights best practices, which can also be applied in any metropolitan jungle that needs intellectual perseverance. Butet shows her intellectual courage, integrity and her sacrifices to become a hero of education. She exercises the intellectual virtues that we all need today to have a healthy mind-set in the pursuit of human rights and dignity. "It is in the minds of men that the defense of peace must be constructed." (UNESCO Constitution)"

Arief Rachman, Professor, Jakarta State University and Executive Chair Indonesian National commission for UNESCO, Indonesian Ministry of Education and Culture

"*The Jungle School* was written by a young woman who is honest, intelligent, creative, courageous, and humble. Butet Manurung has a vision for the future of children's rights—in her case the children of indigenous peoples—to grow and develop within the freedom of their own culture. Her stories are spontaneous, easy to understand and fun to read. We can all learn a great deal from Butet, one of Indonesia's valiant fighters for children's rights."

Kak Seto, Chairman of the Board of Trustees of the National Comission for the Protection of Children

"Here is a book that engages in the same issues as Claude Lévi-Strauss' classic study, *Tristes Tropiques*. It presents the portrait of a fledgling anthropologist who sets out to educate an isolated jungle population in Sumatra on how to deal with the modern world as it threatens to overwhelm them. This learning process works both ways and offers the reader rare insights into another world of living. This is a book to be enjoyed and appreciated."

James J. Fox, Australian National University

"Objectively, the Orang Rimba face insurmountable odds against the rape and pillage of their rainforest home. They are illiterate, have no legal titles to their land, no friends in high places. They reside at the bottom of the Indonesian social totem pole, living a life that might seem idyllic, but which has to face modern threats. Butet Manurung has guts, we can see that by her decision to live with the Orang Rimba in Sumatra. But she also has a dream, that by helping the Orang Rimba become literate and numerate these simple yet sophisticated people will be better able to fight against Big Timber, Big Oil Palm, Big Transmigration, and Big Government to retain control of their tribal lands. It's a brave and imaginative strategy in the type of fight for traditional land rights that I've seen repeatedly in Southeast Asia, notably among the Penan of Borneo. Reading Butet's refreshingly original book I recall Margaret Mead's observation: 'Never doubt that a small group of thoughtful, committed citizens can change the world. Indeed, it is the only thing that ever has.'"

Paul Spencer Sochaczewski, former Head of International Campaigns at WWF, author of Redheads and Soul of the Tiger

"Butet Manurung is your everyday, curious, young urbanite at the helm of an extraordinary adventure. A rare testament of the people we once were, and who still live secretly among us."

Wena Poon, novelist, Prix Hemingway nominee and winner of the Willesden Herald Prize, UK

"With so much of today's news lauding the recent economic success of Indonesia, Butet's experience in the jungle reveals a much less reported story and one that highlights the country's lopsided development. Butet realizes that many are being left behind and that education is the key to their survival in both a literal and figurative sense. As communal conflict spreads and workers take to the streets, her message of self-empowerment is timely and one that cannot be ignored. As an agent of change, Butet has inspired many to follow her example and I hope the readers of this book will also hear the call."

Jason Tedjasukmana, Indonesian Correspondent, TIME Magazine

"Butet gives us a beautiful view of Indonesia. *The Jungle School* is a touching tale of respect, courage, and love for children. I am so looking forward to an awesome film adaptation."

Riri Riza, award-winning Indonesian filmmaker

"A charming and heart-warming book, made more so of course because it opens a window on one of Indonesia's smaller and lesser known indigenous groups."

John McBeth, journalist and author

"Penned with a straightforwardness and utter lack of sentimentalism, *The Jungle School* reveals a powerful voice and a fresh perspective for the reader, a glimpse into the undiscovered customs, traditions, and way of life of the Orang Rimba. Butet Manurung takes us into unmapped territories and dares us to embrace the unknown, to question our differences, our beliefs, and the meaning of civilization through her experience living with the Orang Rimba. The best of authors speak to our hearts and make us feel understood and less alone. Butet opens a door we did not know existed and leaves a lasting impression."

Titania Veda, journalist and former Associate Editor, Jakarta Globe

"Menjaga hutan memang sulit sekali
"Guarding our jungle is really hard

Orang pemerintah saja tak bisa
The goverment can't do it

Apalagi saya yang baru bisa baca tulis dan hitung"
Let alone me who just learned how to read and write"

—Peniti Benang, A SOKOLA Student

A Letter from Deep in the Jungle

It never occurred to me that one day you would be reading my rambling notes. I intended them only for myself. From a very young age, I kept a journal. In it, I complained, expressed my gratitude, my anger, my contentment; I questioned; I complimented; I cursed those who annoyed me. I felt free to unload my feelings without any need to censor or correct them. I felt these candid journals were a little too private to be read by others. I made these notes for myself, casually keeping them tucked in between other books in a cupboard.

By the time I arrived at the Bukit Dua Belas rainforest in Jambi, journal writing was a familiar and constant practice. Typically, during my time in the jungle, I wrote on any paper I could find. Sometimes I wrote on worn-out notebooks, other times on loose pieces of paper jumbled together with teaching materials, or even on the blank side of my students' notes. This enabled me to process ideas from my time with the Orang Rimba. I could also express my anxiety or just scribble a line out of frustration or anger. Quite often, I smugly wrote about issues of which I knew very little.

Later, some of my friends suggested that I publish my notes. They thought that, despite their raw and personal nature, these notes could change peoples' perspective about the Orang Rimba, providing a window into their daily lives at a time when they are still unknown to the outside world. I thought my friends were crazy. It was beyond my imagination that these scribbled disorganized notes and sometimes curses would interest anyone. And then, there was the question of how the Orang Rimba would react. Bah, I was petrified . . .

My friends were insistent and persuasive. In the process, we had many discussions. Eventually, I gave in. I began to believe that publishing my notes might address the many misconceived ideas about the Orang Rimba. Stereotypes would be challenged, including the presumption that tribal communities are either always or never environmentally aware, that the Indonesian government has made ineffective efforts to 'aid' the Orang Rimba, that Non-Governmental Organizations (NGOs) have a thorough understanding of people's needs, or that individuals like me, who socialize closely with tribal communities, are not objective enough because we are too close to the issues and, thus, have a high probability of making mistakes.

In any case, for what it's worth, each journal entry is an attempt to discover some insight into what it means to be human. These notes do not declare who is wrong or right. Instead, they record the actual events and human experiences of the moment. From this I hope that you, as a reader, will see that the Orang Rimba are able to survive just fine without us outsiders—outsiders who have an appetite for material wealth, outsiders who may feel that they know how to decide which way of life is best for the Orang Rimba.

I hope that you, my reader, are able to experience the daily life of the Orang Rimba through this book. I trust I can show you that the Orang Rimba are not what some people say they are and, furthermore, do not necessarily lack what some imagine they need—clothes, religion or a house with four walls. You may even be surprised to learn about the meaning of happiness and well-being through their eyes.

For the Orang Rimba, their life in the jungle is the way they prefer to live. They have everything they need. They have developed a happy and satisfying life with little reliance on material goods. This way of living in the rainforest is increasingly difficult to hold on to; modern life is encroaching and creating a period of intense cultural change. With this change comes a need to develop new skills and learn new concepts. Often, paradoxically, this learning can only be obtained from the outside world.

I hope that you, the reader, will not feel too disconcerted to find parts of the text quite personal, either in point of view or in the language used. This is to be expected as the book is based on my jungle diary. I opted to keep the text close to a diary form because I wanted to maintain the familiar and direct style of a journal and to keep the ideas and observations as authentic as possible. Consequently, you will not find stories of heroism or adventure in this book. Instead, you will find a recollection of everyday events; my baby steps in getting to know the Orang Rimba.

While I visited many different places between 1999 and 2006, this book only includes stories of my experiences in Jambi. These experiences were valuable stepping-stones in my journey with SOKOLA, a close knit and dedicated group of people who work to provide alternative education for tribal communities. From 1999 to 2003, I worked as an education facilitator at WARSI, a local conservation NGO in Jambi. From 2003 to the present, I worked with others to establish SOKOLA. Through this organization, we set up new schools in Indonesia, such as *Sokola Pesisir* (Coastal School) in Makassar, *Sokola Baca Tulis* (School of Reading and Writing) in Wailago on Flores, *Sokola Ketahanan Hidup* (School for Self-Sufficiency) in Aceh, and literacy programs for the Togutil tribe in North Mollucas and for the Kajang tribe in Bulukumba, South Sulawesi. These schools were established between 2004 and 2007. Some schools opened, closed and re-opened, depending upon the availability of financial support, and most are still running today. We also run short-term post-disaster programs for children in places like Garut, Jogjakarta, Bantul, Klaten, Cianjur and West Sumatra.

While this book seeks to be true to my original diary, some liberties have been taken with the text for practical reasons. Only portions of the journal from the first year, for example, have been included. In addition, some text has been edited where the diary entry is so sparse that it is not possible for the reader to make sense of the sequence of events. Repetitive content has also been deleted. And, items of minor importance, although they were written in great detail, were left out to avoid cluttering the main message of the book or possibly disturbing the peace on this earth!

I organized my writing into two sections. The first section resembles my diary. The second is a compilation of conceptual writing on SOKOLA RIMBA, borne out of a long period of reflective gestation from the early days through to today. This was written during a time that nearly drove me mad. Yet, this period led to the subsequent establishment of SOKOLA by the 'rebels' who provided alternative education for tribal communities dealing with change in their environment. Although the second section is a bit shorter than the first, it is a comprehensive write-up reflecting my experiences over a longer span of time, from the second to the seventh year, including my time spent in Jambi and other locations in Indonesia. The last chapter contains my reflections on changes I discovered after having left the rainforest for seven months. This chapter was initially published in the November 2005 edition of National Geographic Indonesia.

Inevitably, I had to mention certain institutions, individuals and groups. They may find some of the text in this book, where it relates to them, rather discourteous. This was not my intention. I felt it was necessary for me to present conflicting perspectives from different sources to explain my own inner battle. I sincerely did not intend in any way to be disrespectful. Honestly, I would like to be able to say, "The writer is not responsible for the contents of this book," because of impulsive comments about a good number of people and institutions. Ahh, if only this book could be fiction. But that is not to be, as it was all very real. Therefore, with a clear conscience, I take full responsibility for what I have written.

Greetings from the Rimba,

Butet Manurung

Acknowledgements

I would like to thank my late father Victor Manurung who always said, "When you give, you are receiving." He is my inspiration. Papa, you will always be in my heart.

My overwhelming gratitude flows to my dear mother, Anar Tiur Samosir, and my three beloved brothers: Leovan Belgianto, Liebe Goklas and Lukki Partogi, the most phenomenal family of the century! They have not only lent me to SOKOLA RIMBA, but they also welcomed SOKOLA RIMBA when we invaded and set up shop in our family home, using two rooms to accommodate SOKOLA's male and female staff. During this time, my younger brothers endured sleeping in the family room in front of the television. They were subject to a coup d'état in their own home. They even bought wholesome food for the SOKOLA members, who had arrived from the field suffering from acute malnutrition. Their help made my workload much lighter.

My family also visited me several times; my mother visited twice. The first time was in 2001 when I was still with WARSI and the second in March 2007. I secretly shed tears of joy when I took her on a four-hour motorcycle journey from the rainforest back to the city. I was proud to show her the fruits of my labor. I feel privileged to have a job I love and a family as decent as they are. I am also grateful for my adorable, dumb, yet loving dogs who, without fail, have welcomed me home for the last twelve years.

I would like to thank my good friends in Team Five SOKOLA: Dodi Rokhdian, Aditya Dipta Anindita, Oceu Apristawijaya and Willy Marlupi. I still become emotional remembering how, only a few years ago, we conceived of this project in the jungle with all our dreams and anxieties. We lived together in poverty, sacrificing all we had just to survive day by day. We had no idea how to realize our dream, but we sensed and believed that this dream was worth fighting for.

I remember how we were so bewildered, aimlessly and anxiously moving back and forth. How much sweat have we dripped on Bukit Dua Belas soil? How much river water have we drunk? How many animals have we devoured? Ha . . . How many times did we have to go to the bathroom out in the open? Hopefully it was not all done in vain.

Remember what Paulo Coelho said in "The Alchemist": "If you truly want something, all the universe conspires in helping you to achieve it." The whole universe lent a hand to help us.

Thank you to Ibu Doctor Herty Herjati for her dedication to her work in caring for and treating the children of the Orang Rimba and to the multi-tasking anthropologist, Stefani Steinebach, who helped us to initiate SOKOLA. They were the ones who helped us realize that dreams without action would simply make us egoists.

A big thanks goes to all the teachers and volunteers of SOKOLA, past and present: Hanoy Handayani, Dila Apristawijaya, Rubby, Icha, Alif, Habibi, Ridha, Ryan, Aday, Anneu, Dian, Susi, Vicko, Agung, Imran, Muhlis, Shanti, Ayu, Efi, Azizah, Puri, Dwi, Fawaz, Deddi, Gimbal, Eva, Thessa, Maway, Ibe, and many others who contributed for several months or helped us with some events, working in diverse areas in Sumatra, Sulawesi, Flores, the Moluccas, and Jakarta. Thank you, all of you, for making the children's smiles a little brighter in the jungle, on the coast, in the slums, among the ruins, in every possible place.

My enormous gratitude goes out to the past and present jungle cadre: Gentar, Linca, Bekilat, Peniti Benang, Penyuruk, Pengendum, Pemilang Laman and Mijak. You are all very special people. Finally, thanks go to WARSI who made it possible for me to fall whole-heartedly in love with the Orang Rimba and gave me the opportunity to learn about and overcome complicated obstacles.

My thanks and great respect are due my supporters: Avi Mahaningtyas, Pak Don Marut, Aca and Pak Sugiono, Mbak Tya Adhitama, Andru and Wiwied Subowo, Atur Manurung and Tulang Bonar Samosir. Special thanks go to my guru, Herry Yogaswara, who taught me what being an anthropologist really means. I hope I will be able to emulate my supporters now and for the rest of my life.

Thank you INSIST and INSIST Press, Pak Toto Rahardjo, Pak Roem Topatimasang, and the late Mansur Faqih, who have relentlessly supported SOKOLA since 2003, even when my own faith in achieving the dream faltered. Thank you to my editor Dodi Yuniar, who helped me clarify my thoughts and put them into words and assisted me in forming the framework and developing an easy-to-read format.

There were times, while turning my journal into a book, when I felt like giving up and I have always had some anxiety abut bringing my private thoughts to the page. Circumstances, like frequent travel on an erratic timetable to places without computer access or electricity, made it difficult for me to write. Yet, I was committed to INSIST, my original publisher, having received a grant to write this book in Indonesian in 2003.

Thank you to the many sponsors who made this book real—so it can be held and read and distributed around the world. I also offer my deep appreciation to everyone who has read and endorsed this book, in both its Indonesian and English versions. You are all such busy people, yet you generously took the time to read my words, write your comments and lend your support.

To my great team who helped with the English edition of the book: Gouri Mirpuri, Anya Robertson, Tiro Daenuwy, Madeleine Maple, Ro King, Cindy Saja thank you so much. No words can express my gratitude. It is astonishing what five tightly scheduled people in different places can accomplish toiling over a labor of love.

A very special thank you goes to my loving husband, Kelvin James Milne, who always supports me for being myself. There are times when I can see your eyes light up as you listen to my dreams and there are times when your criticism grounds me and reinvigorates my strength. Often, you and I believe that we are reincarnated twins from a past life. I love you very much.

Thank you to everyone involved whose name I have not mentioned. And thank you, kind reader, for being interested enough to read this book. Please excuse any omissions.

Enjoy this book. I dedicate it to everyone who has cared for children living in different and difficult circumstances, under extreme conditions or with complexities. I also dedicate it to educators, travelers, and readers who love this earth and its inhabitants. I hope there are parts that enlighten your perspective on tribal communities, including how they perceive themselves.

I pray for all my students in the jungle whom I love. Thank you for your trust and the lessons of life you taught me.

Foreword

This project began with an irresistible phone call. I was doing a book about the ecological heroes of Indonesia. A friend rang me up and said he had the perfect Eco Hero for me to write about. Could he bring his "jungle friend" over for a chat?

What is a "jungle friend"? I wondered. I pictured an Indonesian Indiana Jones. He would show up at our appointed time, slightly dusty from the road. Was he old and leathery, or young and robust? And just what kind of heroic acts did he perform in the jungle?

The Eco Hero, aka Jungle Friend, turned out to be Butet. Butet is a demure young woman. A sweet, wonderful, enlightened soul, the kind one only occasionally meets in a lifetime, but whose ideas, energy and positive aura remain an inspiration for a long time.

The rest of that first afternoon with Butet was spent sitting on the sofa on my patio, and traveling deep, deep into the jungles of Jambi. Butet took me on an adventure with the gentlest and kindest of people, the Orang Rimba. I learnt of their respect for their surroundings and how environmental conservation was cleverly written into their *adat* or traditional practice through a series of taboos. I also came to understand that the carefree, undisturbed lifestyle they have lived for hundreds of years could be under great threat. A threat the Orang Rimba will not possibly be able to fight without help.

Butet and her brave volunteers ensure that all the eleven tribes of the Orang Rimba are armed with the greatest weapon of all—education. With literacy and numeracy. With enhanced life-skills. With a clear knowledge of their rights and their legal standing. With self-respect. And, with a determination to protect their lands, their lives, their life-style.

Literacy will help them face the outside world, which has suddenly turned up uninvited at their doorsteps. The Orang Rimba need to understand the words on the papers they sign, so they don't get cheated anymore. They need numbers to calculate how much they should be paid for resin or rubber when trading, and literacy to read the laws that protect them and their forests. Most of all, they need to understand the language of the outsider so they can face that world bravely and on equal footing.

It is because of people like Butet, and their literacy efforts, that young Orang Rimba can now confront illegal loggers. Imagine the logger's astonishment when an Orang Rimba comes up to him, flourishing a legal document and citing the rights of their people "according to Article 21 of the constitution"—now that is progress!

There are currently five SOKOLA throughout Indonesia bringing literacy to indigenous people living in areas too remote to access formal education. Butet and her determined young volunteers live their lives with the people they are helping, whom they have grown to love.

I began the task of translating Butet's diary two years ago from Indonesian to English. I worked with my fantastic team of Anya, Ro, Tiro, Cindy and Madeline. We now want the outside world to read these remarkable stories and go on the same journey that we have gone on, deep into the jungles of Jambi with the gentle Rimba. For only when their stories are read will their voices be heard. And only then will their cry for recognition and respect be understood.

Gouri Mirpuri
Author and Activist
Jakarta, January 2012

Part 1

First Days in the Rainforest

Chapter 1

First Days in the Jungle

September 24, 1999
My first day of "work"

I can't say this is my first day of work. I dislike that word. Let's call this my first day of living!

These are the words I say to myself while travelling by bus from Rawamangun terminal in Jakarta towards Bangko in the Province of Jambi. Bangko is located between Sarolangun and Muaro Bungo as you travel towards Padang on the island of Sumatra, so my bus will travel by road as well as by ferry.

"The journey from Jakarta to Bangko will take between twenty-two and twenty-six hours," says the ALS bus driver. ALS stands for Antar Lintas Sumatera (Trans-Sumatran Highway). My friends jokingly call it Antar Langsung Surga (The Heaven Express) because the bus is driven so fast and in such a seemingly careless manner that you feel as if you are one step away from death.

My bus journey takes so many hours. It is unbearable. And it is boring. I have nothing to do but stare out the window at the road, daydream or sleep. "Is Bangko still far away?" I ask the conductor.

It is the third time I have asked this question and it begins to annoy him. His previous answer was "still far". This time it is, "I can't say *Mbak*, we will get there tomorrow!!"

I don't dare ask him again. I resume my alternate pattern of daydreaming and sleeping until I hear the conductor yell, "Bangko, Bangko!" I'm startled. "What? Oh, finally . . ."

I start to collect my bags but oh no! My cool sneakers had slipped out of reach when I took them off. The driver and conductor are getting angry because the bus has stopped for quite some time while I still have my bum in the air and my head down. I crawl beneath the seats looking for my shoes.

I finally leave the bus, hastily hauling down my two bags and dropping them on the side of the road as I grumble to myself. Damned *Batak*. They are so rude. How could he just drop me off like that? I know it's Bangko but where do I go next? And the bus takes off with my left shoe!

People stare at me with amusement, especially when they see that I am only wearing one shoe. I look for the nearest store and to this day I can clearly remember its name, *Toko Obat Bangko Permai* (Bangko Permai Drug Store). I unpack my bags, take out my sandals, and search for my acceptance letter from WARSI with their phone number. I find the number, then use the store's phone to call WARSI for my pick up. The WARSI driver arrives shortly. He is quite friendly, but once I hear his foreign accent, I think to myself, "He's probably of Malay descent."

We drive to the WARSI office, only a hundred meters away from the Sumatran Highway. I am quite impressed by the town. I had expected that everything, including the office, was going to be deep in the jungle. I had already packed some washing detergent and all my personal necessities because I thought there wouldn't be any stores around. I certainly wasn't expecting a town.

The WARSI office looks like a house. It's pretty cool. One by one the WARSI staff introduce themselves to me, each with a dismissive smile. I am beginning to feel uncomfortable because they are acting so formal. With an introduction like this, I know things are going to be a little tense. I am really impatient and just want to get into the jungle. The tour of the office feels like a real estate agent's presentation of a house. Each division is allocated a room. There is the natural resources room, the human resources room and the data room, which is for maps and other research material. The remainder of the office is used for administration. It is all extremely pedantic.

The first question I am asked is, "So you're the one who wants to be a secretary, is that right?" They were looking for new employees for two positions—a secretary for the office and an anthropologist to work as an education facilitator in the jungle.

I answer, "No, I'm the education facilitator." The person who asked the question looks surprised. He says, "Really? But you're so skinny. Are you sure you're strong enough? Have you ever been to a tropical rainforest?" I stay silent, not answering the question.

I sit and wait in the office for the rest of the day. The WARSI staff barely take the time to sit down and chat with me. I feel ignored, but maybe they are just too busy. Their standard response, when they hear that I am there to take up the education facilitator position is "Oh really?

Are you strong enough? Have you ever been in the jungle? Are you afraid of the dark?" I boastfully answer that I have climbed the peak of Trikora in Papua, six years ago. Their attitude toward me does not change. I finally meet the director of WARSI. After working through several things, I am shown to my accommodations nearby, provided by WARSI for all their employees.

I will stay in the staff residence for women. There are four of us, an anthropologist, a secretary, a treasurer and myself. I have never before lived with work colleagues. My only other experience living with people, other than my family, was sharing a house with several friends during college.

This residential experience with my WARSI colleagues turns out to be quite different from my college days. Formerly, in my shared student house, everyone would pool whatever we had. When someone cooked, it was for the entire house. If someone had a snack, he or she would offer to share it with others. I slowly become aware that this communal style of living is unacceptable in the WARSI women's residence. At first, working on the assumption that the women will be sharing food, I snack on food I find in the kitchen. I become most unpopular, even though the other women still offer to share food out of politeness. Eventually, it becomes an embarrassment to even accept these polite offers of food. There is just one exception to the no sharing rule—we split the rice bill.

Each woman cooks only for herself! I know that living together can be so much easier and efficient if everyday activities are shared. For example, we could take turns cooking. But, maybe we all have different tastes. As for me, I will eat anything. I begin to cook my own meals and often become annoyed with this time-consuming arrangement. For example, there are timing issues, such as having access to the small number of bowls when I need them. I begin to eat out frequently. I borrow the office motorcycle. Voila! Hunger solved. In my spare time, I watch movies, read, and write. I think to myself, "Why make life so difficult?"

October 13, 1999
My first encounter with the Orang Rimba

Until I depart for the jungle, I think my journey to the Orang Rimba will be like the brief mountain wilderness hiking trips that I have enjoyed with my friends. We hiked until we were drenched in sweat, climbing all the way to the top of the mountain, then all the way back again, tumbling down the mountain side. There was never anything extraordinary in these trips. The mountains were always there and I was always planning my next hiking trip.

We start towards our destination, speeding onward in a jeep. Our group consists of five people: the driver, the WARSI Director, the WARSI media specialist, the WARSI anthropologist Amilda Sani and me. Amilda has more than two years of work experience with programs associated with the Orang Rimba. She is assigned to chaperone me during my first two-month visit to the rainforest. The Director and the media specialist are going to check on a WARSI project, an eco-tourism hut just outside the jungle. Well, actually, I think WARSI wants to check on project expenditures. Whoa, don't be so cynical Butet!

Throughout the journey, every question I ask is answered with a story. I begin to wonder what it is the Rimba are like. What kind of job will this be? I never imagined that helping to educate an indigenous tribe could be classified as a job. Honestly, there is nothing else I would rather do!

The jeep ride is quite bumpy as we drive along the rutted and uneven trail. "I hope the place is nice," I think to myself. I begin to reminisce about my adventures in the wilderness. My friends and I were constantly attracted to exploring exotic corners of Indonesia. We were "Nature's children". We considered ourselves true nature lovers because we deeply enjoyed visiting these places. We always felt this great satisfaction when we let go of our egos in the presence of Nature, almost revelling in the fatigue and discomfort of a strenuous trek.

Walking in the wilderness held a range of delights for us. The wonder of mountain peaks pointing towards the skies, brooding caves with unknown creatures lurking inside, steep cliffs beckoning us to climb and the unforgiving, menacing river rapids taunting and seducing us. Above our heads, we had the unending azure sky and beyond, the enigmatic sapphire waters of the ocean. Ahh, there are so many places on the planet with breathtakingly beautiful natural horizons. I cannot express how lucky I feel to be alive.

For me this feeling of intense pleasure, in response to being in the natural wilderness, is present in every journey. A feeling that cannot be expressed in words. It is a weird passion, a burst of energy that flows under the routine of everyday life. As nature lovers, we identify with the drama of the wild seen in nature photography and with the stories of heroism and adventure in the wilderness. These images and stories reinforce our desire to be special. In particular, we value and seek to express the qualities we so admire, such as courage, strength, and self-confidence. This is always in our minds when we hike in the natural wilderness.

Nature summons us with her tantalising whispers. We return, satisfied momentarily, and then plan for another trip unable to be truly satisfied or content without her delights, energy and inspiration. It is like an addiction. It makes sense to call us 'nature junkies' instead of 'nature lovers'.

I finally meet them!

And finally, I meet them, these people called the Orang Rimba. We arrive at the edge of the rainforest at the southern end of the Bukit Dua Belas National Park. I realize it is WARSI practice to introduce newcomers by saying they would like to learn about the customs of the Orang Rimba. The Orang Rimba don't seem to have a problem with this because WARSI has already helped them in many ways. We also meet up with our co-worker, Tijok, at the eco-tourism hut he had built.

The Orang Rimba

The Orang Rimba community is spread throughout the 60,000-hectare Bukit Dua Belas National Park. I learn that the name Bukit Dua Belas, or Twelve Hills, does not literally mean that there are twelve hills in this tropical rainforest. It just means that the hills form twelve perpendicular rows called *setali bukit* by the Orang Rimba. The Orang Rimba believe that gods, demons, and djinns dwell within the hills of the Park.

The Park covers three regions: Batang Hari, Muaro Tebo and Sarolangun, and there are about eleven *Temenggung* or chiefs. Based on a 1997 WARSI survey there are 1,300 Orang Rimba in the Park. Each *rombong* or group area is named after its closest associated river. I first visit the area called the Tengkuyungon River *rombong*.

Until this point, I have only seen two Rimba men. The first is Cerinay, about 20 years old, who leads us down a track for half an hour. The other is a 40-year-old named Ngandun (*Bepak* Terenong), who has just returned from hunting and driving off a group of illegal loggers. He speaks to our Director in Malay, who in turn nods his head in agreement, as if noting down these things in his head.

I wonder why my Director isn't taking notes. Maybe it is just my college student brain. I write anything down, even if I don't really know what it means. I also have no idea what my Director is going to do with this information. Is he gathering data? It doesn't seem that it is possible for him to confront illegal loggers himself? Or maybe, he can use his authority to identify these illegal loggers for the Forestry Department? Or, perhaps the Governor? Ahh . . . I don't think it matters. It's not as if they can really do anything about it. So documenting and archiving data is only of secondary concern, which makes sense if he wants to stay in his comfort zone.

Then, along come Ngandun's wife, *Indok* Terenong, and their daughter Bemulo. They shelter behind *Bepak* Terenong and look at us like we are aliens. Amilda starts to talk in the Rimba language. I try to listen to their conversation using my 100-word Indonesian—Rimba pocket dictionary Ahh . . . it's too fast and unclear. I can't follow the conversation.

I observe *Indok* Terenong's attire. I have seen photographs of the Orang Rimba and heard stories about them from my friends at the office, yet I am startled to see a bare-chested woman. In the jungle, married Orang Rimba females do not cover their chests. It's more practical because they are often breast-feeding their children.

At first, I am embarrassed looking at *Indok* Terenong's bare chest. I glance over at my male colleagues, but they seem indifferent. I suddenly feel ignorant and arrogant, confronted with my own prejudice, assuming that my way of dress is somehow more dignified than this backward and obscene attire. I remind myself that I need to be non-judgmental, humble and willing to accept every single 'oddity' with an open mind. I realize this will be the only way to understand them.

Bemulo, the eight-year-old girl is adorable. She has long black hair and her arms are covered in silver bangles. She is wearing about ten colorful, beaded necklaces, hanging around her neck and chest. One of the necklaces is a simple thread looped through a coin showing Queen Wilhelmina's face. I greet Bemulo with my most sincere smile and a look that says, "Please take me with you to play in your jungle." I then purposely ignore her when she too shows interest, hoping that this will spark her curiosity further. That is my mother's way of getting acquainted with children. Once her mother sees the interaction, she responds with a smile.

I see many things that day. I am a bit disappointed because the rainforest isn't as beautiful as I had imagined it. I think to myself, "How is it possible that people live here in this awful place?" I then remember what a friend told me.

"Tet, there are many people who say that they like children. This may be just a superficial interest, untested until meeting a child with green snot dripping out of their nose, with tangled, dirty hair, a child who hasn't bathed in days, or one who is crying uncontrollably. It is only when we meet this child that we can see whether we still genuinely care. When you say you love, then you must love unconditionally. I get teary eyed when I see children trying to be strong. On the other hand, when I see children crying because they are spoiled, I feel like hitting their parents on the head."

I hope I'm not like that. I hope I am not just superficially responding to what I see.

In the jungle

I think to myself, many people call themselves nature lovers, but do they care about the deforestation of these jungles? Will they still travel and explore the rainforest once it is spoiled? Or, do they care about the filthy Ciliwung River in Jakarta? What about the waste that keeps piling up on its banks? Do they care that the Pulo Gadung bus station is suffocating with pollution from cars? What about vegetables that are full of pesticides?

Oh God, what have I been doing all this time? I have twice helped people whose homes were flooded in Tasikmalaya and South Bandung. I felt so proud of my efforts. But, the aid came from the universities, not from me. That's all I did. Why did I stop there? Why did I not do more than that? How can I have been so self-centered all this time?

I observe the Orang Rimba and their surroundings. I wonder to myself, are we in the rainforest or is this just re-growth or brushwood? It is not interesting at all. Maybe it only looks like this because of the close proximity to the village? Maybe it gets better deeper in the jungle? Why is this river so narrow? Why are there flies and mosquitoes everywhere? There are so many bald patches in the rainforest. These are previously cultivated fields now littered with fallen trees. It is so ugly.

But then I realize if the tropical rainforest were still beautiful and healthy, I need not be here. The beauty is a sign that there are no problems in the rainforest. Why am I really here? I cannot imagine what sort of education best fits their needs. Ahh . . . I have no clue. Will they even want education? Do they need it?

When they look at me, they seem disinterested. Just then, an angel intercepts the rambling demon inside my brain, "You know, Tet, it is

31

in this "ugly" jungle and among these "ugly" children you are needed most. Come on, you are just being tested!"

Day turns slowly into night, and we stay at the eco-tourism hut built by Tijok. He is the person in charge of developing eco-tourism here. The hut is very cozy. It is just like a shack in the paddy fields, only wider by about four to six meters. The pillars are made from tree branches ten to twenty centimeters in diameter and the roof is covered in *rumbai* leaves. The hut is partially walled; there are bamboo mats for the floor and an attractive set of stairs leading down to the river. Everything is matched perfectly in rattan—it's quite adorable.

Everyone chats into the night. I, on the other hand, write quietly and peer around now and then, like a confused person needing help. I know I must look dumb.

Today feels long. "What happened today?" I ask myself. The rainforest and the strange people I am assigned to educate seem to consume my soul. I am slowly separating myself from my comfortable and pleasant life. Silhouettes of my mother and my little brother appear in my head. My mind also wanders to thoughts about my boyfriend and the movie theaters in Jakarta.

I love watching movies. I wonder what movies are playing right now? I remember my friends in Bandung riding their motorbikes around town in the afternoon. I think of my favorite snack, *batagor*, those fried fish and tofu croquettes at Simpang Dago. Ahh . . . I try refocusing; I can daydream later. Once again, the nature junkie and the urban enthusiast clash.

Will I really enjoy the rainforest and the Orang Rimba? I am filled with doubt, but at least today there were two Rimba females who noticed me and smiled. That was refreshing, like an oasis in a desert. I do not want to draw conclusions too quickly. I wonder if I should start work on a job as crazy as this. Crazy in the sense that my lifestyle is flipped completely upside down. Crazy because I have absolutely no clue about what I will be doing.

I decide to start by bathing. Then cleaning, cooking, gathering fire wood, starting a fire, making sure the flames don't blow out, and so on. This is not so bad after all; it's actually quite entertaining. Being here feels like I am stuck in that movie *The Gods Must Be Crazy*. I was lucky to have learnt how to live in the wilderness from my comrades at PALAWA UNPAD, the nature lovers' club at Padjadjaran University in Bandung. I didn't do too badly during those twenty days of boot camp in the mountains. At least I'm not too urbanized. I'm used to eating bush food and being here is just like camping for me.

October 17, 1999
Orang Rimba = nature lovers

I start to become accustomed to the rhythm of life in the jungle and I begin to notice the beauty of the Orang Rimba. Things I see every day bring about this new appreciation: a little child, about four years old, adept at tree climbing; a mother, digging down through a meter of soil to harvest *benor* (a wild tuber) from the ground; two men climbing a honey tree; girls bathing in the river using rocks as their 'natural' soap; a girl weaving *rumbai* leaves to make a mat. I become aware that the Rimba are complaining about the receding rainforest and about the slow loss of rainforest resources. Ahh . . . I'm embarrassed. Aren't they the nature lovers, not me? Look! They really know how to appreciate Mother Nature.

Several friends have told me how the Orang Rimba collect honey. So, I am excited to be invited to harvest honey with two Orang Rimba families. The honey tree is located a long way off. We walk at a slow pace from morning until dusk. The path we take leads us to the sacred *sialang* tree, which towers above the jungle canopy with great majesty. Here, the natural jungle can be appreciated because of its dense vegetation. However, I still see small clearings with remnants of tree trunks cut by chainsaws, probably by illegal loggers.

The honey tree is special. It has a powerful presence. It is elegant, proud and majestic. At night, its white branches are florescent. More than forty meters tall, it is considered to be the tallest tree in the rainforest. The many beehives entwined in its branches add to the tree's aura.

As I look up from the base of this tree, the beehives and the leaves seem to be smiling at my insignificance while seductively inviting me to touch them. It is amazing. I am happy to see that such trees still exist in the tropical rainforest.

For the Orang Rimba, the *sialang* tree is sacred. It is handed down as an inheritance; usually the daughter inherits ownership of the tree. If there is more than one daughter, then all the girls receive a share. Chopping down this tree is completely prohibited by tribal law. The customary fine for such an act is very high and is usually paid in hundreds of lengths of *koin* or traditional cloth. At twenty thousand rupiah per piece of *koin*, this equates to a whopping ten million rupiah fine. This fine is not sufficient to protect the *sialang* tree because it has a high alternative value as a forestry product. The price per cubic meter of wood can range from seven hundred thousand to two million rupiah.

(Note that in 1999, US$1 = Rp. 15,000, so the value of the wood would be between US$50 and $150 per cubic meter.)

The Orang Rimba harvest honey not just for immediate consumption; they can store honey for years. Once collected, the honey is cooked and then the liquid is poured into bottles or large tin cans and sealed shut. Every member of the family, even the children, receives a share of honey in a small plastic bottle. Honey owned by a family is stored in larger containers. The honey can be eaten raw or mixed with warm water and drunk. It can also be eaten with boiled sweet potatoes or cassava . . . yummy! The Rimba also sell the honey to city dwellers for Rp. 6,000 per liter. This price is below the outside market value, which ranges between Rp. 10,000 and Rp. 15,000.

We immediately set up temporary shelters around the *sialang* trees selected for harvesting. Our shelters consist of six branches collected from small trees to be used as poles. One end of each branch is pushed into the ground and the branches are simply shaped to create the shelter. Other shelters use existing trees with a plastic tarp to create a roof. If we had more time, and felt industrious, we could have made shelters with leaf-thatched roofs. These are more comfortable because the materials used lower the indoor temperature and last longer.

To harvest the honey, these towering honey trees pointing straight into the sky, must first be climbed. Climbing pegs *(lantak)*, made from the hard wood called *pisang*, are used to create steps.

First, the small pegs are all sharpened at one end with a knife. They are then driven into the trunk of the tree with a mallet made out of a stronger wooden material. The pegs are arranged like a staircase from the bottom to the top of the tree. Once the staircase is in place the harvest climb begins.

It is the shaman who first climbs the tree. It is said that the bees are singing angels. I feel an eerie shudder when the shaman begins to chant. The chant is part of an exorcism ritual designed to drive away the dark wood spirits of the tree. As the chant continues, a growing spiritual air prevails and the harvest proceeds. I have no clue what he is saying, but I can feel the vibrations of his tone resonating deep in my bones.

> *Dua lah tiga kidding tegentung*
> Two, three rattan baskets hang
> *Kiding kecil diisi padi*
> The small basket filled with rice

Dua tiga bujang tekampung
> Two, three bachelors leave the jungle to settle

Seorang tidak menolong kanti, adek ooo iii . . .
> Nobody helps me, oh darling, nooo . . .

The *sialang* tree must be persuaded to shoo away its dark wood spirits. It is only then that the Orang Rimba are allowed to taste the honey that the gods have sent them. If the tree spirits do not leave, they will push the climber off the tree when he reaches the top. There are said to have been cases where the climber has just disappeared. If something like this were going to happen, warning omens would be heard, either by someone near the harvest or by a relative far away. These ominous signs usually come in the form of sounds from a particular bird, often in a dream.

After the exorcism ritual comes the placement of the *lantak*. The climber creates a staircase up the tree using the *lantak*, all the while singing a particular song. This song persuades the *induk rapah* or queen bee not to attack and sting the climbers during harvest. This "persuasion song" is particularly unusual. The song uses romantic imagery with sensual elements in a verse form, like a lover's serenade to a girl. These songs also use poetic devices such as rhyme, rhythm and metaphor and have a strong musical quality. The lyrics below are a record of my understanding of the verses at the time and not a direct translation.

Orang Kerinci mati semalam
> A Kerinci man died last night

Mati ditanam di bawah Kandis
> Died and was buried under the Kandis tree

Elok nian mimpi semalam
> What a wonderful dream it was last night

Mimpi memeray susu gediy
> Dreams of milking a virgin's breast

Harvesting honey is best done at night. So, Amilda and I observe the harvest from underneath the tree in the early hours of the morning, around two a.m. We become close friends; especially after an army of venomous *selembedo* ants swarm my legs. Their bite feels like an electric shock. I freak out and jump around in a panic, which makes everyone laugh. I am happy if my misfortune makes them friendlier toward me!

They tell me to just move out of the path of the poisonous ants. There are thousands of them.

At the beginning of each climb, we notice the intense determination of the climber as he climbs further and further up the tree. We stop looking while we arrange some dry branches to sit on the wet ground. I wonder where the climber is as I look up into pitch darkness. Occasionally, I see embers falling from the *tunom*. They fall and fizzle out before they hit the ground. It is nice to watch, just like fireworks during New Year's Eve at Monas, the National Monument in central Jakarta. I grow tired, as it is now two-thirty in the morning. I sit with my arms wrapped around my knees. As I rest my head on my knees I begin, like a tired child, to lean against one of the mothers in the group. I lean my back on hers and she doesn't mind. I am so happy. She doesn't mind touching me.

Soon, I hear a voice shouting, "Take this wooden bucket!" The bucket descends just like a pail being lowered into a well. We cheer as we receive our first batch of honey. The bucket is full of honeycombs oozing with honey in which bee larvae wriggle like white worms. This is pure honey. They call the larvae *rapah* and the people say they taste like milk. This analogy really makes me curious because drinking cow's milk or any milk from a domesticated animal is taboo for the Orang Rimba.

Bemulo, the little girl, offers me a *rapah*. I cannot believe that I am being asked to eat larvae. I examine it closely. The others are fighting to get a taste of the delicacy. "It's sooo good," they say.

"*Cubo!! Beyikk!*" "Try it! It's good!" she says.

I take the worm and hold it with two fingers. I examine the small critter, and then look at the mother and daughter in disbelief. They are smiling at me in a mischievous way. I think to myself, "All right, there's nothing to it, just try it." I swallow it in one big gulp. "Thank God," I think, "glad that's over with." Then, I am offered the next one. It is so disgustingly slimy as it slips down my throat. I swallow it quickly. Gleck! They keep offering me more. *Aduh!* I eventually get used to the taste.

At the end of the harvest, I am given honey to carry back and allowed to take as much as I can carry. Amilda and I have two small bottles we use for cooking oil and mineral water. We fill the bottles. I am quite proud to be carrying honey that I removed from the comb by myself.

October 18, 1999
Seeking refuge

Soon, we find ourselves running away from the fury of the stinging bees. The bees only stop chasing us once we jump into the river. We seek refuge from the angry honeybees in the river for quite some time. It is dawn before we dare to return to our shelter. I want to just return to camp across the river, but I remember that all our belongings are in the shelter by the *sialang* tree.

My clothes, now wet and sticking to my skin, are no protection from the cold. I am also hungry. And I don't even have the small knife I use to remove leeches.

Leeches are now prolific, increasing with the start of the rainy season. We are being bitten all over. Amilda and I take turns removing the leeches from each other's backs. They start off thin as a needle, but then expand to the size of a little finger without me even noticing them. Madness! On Java, I would never allow myself to be in crazy situations like this. I am probably dealing with more than forty leeches. I will run out of blood if this keeps up, I think to myself. I'm already skinny as it is, what will be left of me if my blood is drained to the very last drop?

October 19, 1999
Fishing

A day after our escape from the bees, I ready my backpack. I pack snacks, my small knife, a notebook and a pen. I am ready to write down whatever is on my mind with my pen and to slay leeches with my knife. From now on, intent on revenge, I will kill all the leeches that dare attach themselves to my body. I will kill them in cold blood or pull their ends in opposite directions, "tsssp!" until they tear apart!

At noon, at our new campsite, the women of the group, *Indok* Terenong and her three daughters: Rantai, Ngali and Bemulo, along with Amilda and I, go to the river to look for fish. I park myself on the riverbank to observe them from afar. I notice the cuts on my calf are beginning to show signs of infection. I think that this may be due to malnutrition and a lack of protein in my diet. I am worried that I might become ill if I follow them into the muddy water to fish.

The name of the river is Aek Behan. It is beautiful. There are many monkeys in the tall trees above me and the birds are chirping along with the crickets. Fish and other marine animals swim back and forth.

I have the urge to document all of this. I begin to write; recording the events I have not had a chance to write about in the days before.

October 21, 1999
Back to "civilization"

Today Amilda has to return for official leave, so I return with her to Kabupaten. As we leave the rainforest I am surprised to learn that the Orang Rimba are being hired and paid as guides and porters. In one day, they earn between Rp. 10,000 and Rp. 15,000 for this short-term work.

October 25, 1999
Back to the jungle again, alone

I return to the rainforest, to the cassava fields in Tengkuyungon. WARSI did not want me to return to the jungle by myself. The usual practice is for new staff members to be accompanied during their first three months of working in the jungle. I want to try to go alone, as I am becoming quite close to the family that I went honey harvesting with, especially with their daughters.

I leave with a WARSI team and the 10th grade students from SMA Xaverius II, Jambi, who are participating in the Environmental Culture education program that Tijok designed. Their high school teachers incorporate this program into their biology class.

Jealousy

My hut is located about a fifteen minutes walk from the group because I am not allowed to live in close proximity to the Orang Rimba for fear that I might spread disease. Living alone in the rainforest turns out to be quite overwhelming. There is no one to act as a translator. I have no one to talk to because of the language barrier. I eventually find that I can chat with Cerinay, who speaks Malay, which is similar to Indonesian. My conversations with Cerinay get me into deep trouble. One afternoon, in the middle of a chat, his wife confronts me with a long spear pointed directly at me.

"I'll spear you! You lying outsider! You said you wanted to do research, but it turns out that you want to steal somebody's husband! I'm going to spear you to death!"

She is crying and talking very fast, all at the same time. I cannot understand what is wrong. I only know that she is mad at me. The only part that I understand is "you want to steal somebody's husband." She thinks that I am going to take her husband. Seriously!? No thanks!

I am so confused. Cerinay then translates for me what his wife is saying. I apologize right away. I did not think that our innocent conversations would have this effect. Cerinay also apologizes for his wife's behavior. Cerinay and I try to explain that I am only talking with him because I have trouble with their language. Finally she calms down, but I am not entirely sure that she isn't still mad at me.

The three of us speak calmly together, but it feels awkward. Cerinay, being the peacemaker, asks his wife to accompany me to my hut, while he returns to his. I refuse, still a bit worried that she might spear me in the middle of the night. It is not until later that I realize that the Orang Rimba would never do such a thing. I ask them to leave me alone, convincing them that I am used to being alone in the jungle. Yeah right! Cerinay's wife looks like she is sorry, but I prefer being alone to being with a person who might still harbor ill feelings toward me.

They begin to leave, but hesitate. Worried for my safety, Cerinay gives me a short lesson on how to defend myself from bears and evil people or ghosts who might call my name. I am also taught how to use a huge machete or a sharp wooden branch to kill or trap a snake. Cerinay's wife just watches quietly. It is seven-thirty in the evening and I am starting to think he may have just wanted to scare me.

It is quite late by the time I get home. Being alone in the middle of the jungle starts to scare me. The animal noises are especially alarming. They are more varied and louder than those I am used to from my student trips to the mountains. I remember that I encountered several illegal loggers one recent afternoon. What if they happen to wander by and see that I'm alone? Oh . . . now, what is that mantra to make me disappear? Does it really work? I must learn it.

I lay down, still holding on to my spear, and I pray. This is, perhaps, the most genuine prayer of my life. I try to sleep, but it is too difficult. The many mosquitoes do not make it any easier. I begin to fantasize in this dreadful atmosphere. What if I fall asleep and a bear or tiger attacks? Which would cause more pain? Being mauled by a bear or bitten by a tiger? I finally build up enough courage to sit up. I take a piece of paper and begin writing letters to my loved ones. One of the letters is for my beloved mother. This is the first letter I have written to her from the jungle:

Dear Mother,

I'm so sorry I forced you to allow me to work here. By tomorrow, I will have been eaten by a bear or a tiger. I want to let you know that I love you and I do not regret what I have done.

With love,
Butet

Even as I write this, my heart is saying, "I really regret this!" If I were to really die, ah, that would be so ridiculous, what kind of crazy job is this? That proves that my friends who work in this jungle are also undeniably crazy. The only difference is, I am certainly more unfortunate.

I sleep with my pen clutched in my hand and the spear by my side. I sleep like a log, perhaps because I am exhausted from taking the High School students through the jungle the whole morning. Suddenly, I hear someone scream, *"Bontet!"* Ah, that name. That's what they call me, ever since our first encounter. Maybe they have heard my name wrong, or mispronounce it, or they just happen to like ruining other people's names.

It is a group of little kids and a young girl. *"Kamia tiba, ado mikay ketakuton siyoh?"* "We have arrived, are you scared here?" I understand what she means. I nod happily, and then go back to sleep. In my sleep, I mumble, "Mom, I didn't die today! I still have time to repay your kindness."

That night, I dream of tying Cerinay's wife to a tree.

October 26, 1999
Baptized as an Orang Rimba

This morning *Bepak* Terenong's family brings me to their *genah*, a small hamlet of three to ten huts. I don't understand why, but they ask me to live with them. I am so happy. They are in disbelief when I tell them I do not have enough food to eat for the next few days. I do this on purpose to try and break down some barriers. I share a hut with their daughters, Ngali and Rantai. The leader of this small *rombong* apologizes for the previous night's mishap. He blames Cerinay's wife, as they understand that I am not fluent in Rimba. He also apologizes for not teaching me, when I first arrived, the ways of the jungle, their customs or their language.

Looking back on the day, I feel like I have been baptized as an Orang Rimba. I feel an overwhelming sense of euphoria and forget about all the past tensions. The only thing that dampens my enthusiasm is the head lice I pick up by sharing a room with the girls. These lice tiptoe out of my hair when I lie down in the television room at the WARSI female residence. I have been busy all day trying to kill them to prevent my friends from finding out. I am embarrassed to think that they might assume I always had lice, not understand that I was exposed to them only recently while in the rainforest. While I am having fun exploring every patch of my head to kill lice and making my hair all messy, a friend catches me. She laughs hysterically "You've got fleas, haven't you?"

I see *Bepak* Terenong carrying a *bejuku*, a type of giant tortoise that he places into an *ambung*, a traditional hand-made basket. He laughs with glee and is very proud of what he carries. He yells something that I don't quite understand, but I know what he means. A group of young children come running to greet him, dancing with joy. A long whining sound comes from the spear as it pierces the eye of the giant tortoise. Then follows a loud *"thwack!"* as they open the poor *bejuku's* shell. I see blood spilling out. A drop of blood splatters on my cheek. In a panic, I wipe my face with a small leaf, and throw it away.

This is the first time I witness "murder" in the jungle. A child jeers at me, his bloodied finger pointing toward me as he laughs at my fear. It is sad to see the *bejuku* breathe his last breath while his heart is still pulsing. The poor thing, he does not last much longer. Soon after, he is cooked, and his meat actually tastes pretty good.

This afternoon, I see a dog being buried, even though it isn't yet dead. That's how they treat dying creatures. His name was Juntak. They said that someone in the village gave the dog to them. *"Mr. Juntak is from Medan!"* Oh, I then understand, they probably mean Simanjutak, a *Batak* clan name. Bah! Because I am the only *Batak*, I grin hearing this rather strange name for a dog. What if the members of the Simanjutak clan hear about this?

Juntak was a smart dog who could track down wild game. He ate cassava everyday. They say that he died because he drank from the rivers that had been poisoned by the villagers fishing upstream. It's a pity that only the Orang Rimba can tell there is danger from the change in smell and color of the polluted river. Juntak didn't know. *Indok* Terenong comes with a plastic bag, says something to the dying Juntak, and then places him in the sack while sobbing. Even in sadness, she manages to smile at me. I feel like going to the village upstream to catch the polluter, and then submerging him for two days and two nights in

41

the poisonous water. He would not need to be killed like Juntak; he just needs to experience the same burning sensation on his skin and body.

I feel sad. Yes, losing something that is good is always heart breaking. I knew Juntak was a special dog, even though we'd only met two weeks earlier when he joined us in the rainforest for the honey harvest. I saw how dedicated he was to the family, always loyally accompanying his master, looking for wild game in the jungle. He was a hunting dog. He had caught many wild boars, deer, mouse deer and other animals with his master.

He was a hunting dog, not an *"änjing penjilat burit"* or quite literally a living bottom wipe. The term bottom-licking dog is actually quite descriptive. The Orang Rimba never defecate into the river, instead they dig a hole in dense jungle where people don't pass. A bottom-licking dog is a cleaner; he licks up the mess on babies' bottoms after they defecate. Mothers call the bottom-licking dogs saying, *"Food!!"* Mother and dog have a mutually beneficial relationship—she does not have to clean up the mess, and the dog gets to eat. Very nutritious! Yuck, gross.

October 27, 1999
Magical powers

It is very difficult to find an opening, even a small insight into understanding the Orang Rimba's views on education. Just one wrong move can ruin the relationship that so far is doing great. On this visit, I get a rare chance to understand a little about the Rimba's views on education through their world of poetry.

When they sing their Rimba songs, I record them with a cassette recorder, and then rewrite the words at night. By the morning, I can sing with them together. Of course, I cannot memorize everything. I can only sing along using the words I have written down. In one case, there were over thirty lines of prose in a single Rimba song. How I manage to sing along makes them curious.

"Bontet seketi." "Butet has magic powers." *"Bontet lah menjedi Urang Rimba! Nye doroy tokang legu rimba!"* "Butet has become an Orang Rimba! She has quickly mastered our songs!"

They ask me how I learn to sing so quickly and accurately. I explain the function of the tape recorder and writing. They ask, *"Ertinye, kalu akeh tokang menuley, akeh depot tuliy segelo pantun? Legu? Mentera?"* "If you are good at writing, can you write down poems? And songs? And mantras?" There are no further requests, nor any questions regarding my curious ability. It probably is not yet the right time.

Sometimes, when the children set a mouse deer trap, I draw it and add a description underneath. They examine my drawings then they ask me to draw other things. So I draw something else and then ask them to name the drawing. They soon begin to draw. I happily give them the pencils and pens that I brought along in my bag. They are so excited with these new tools they immediately start to draw all the things they like. For those that do not get a pencil, I show them how to draw on the ground with a stick.

The way they hold the pencils is still rather awkward. But they quickly and successfully mimic my way of holding a pencil. Soon, they draw whatever objects they find interesting. Oddly enough, they only draw objects that surround them. I am amazed at their skill in portraying animals in pictures. Even though I am not an expert in art, I am surprised that they have such a good sense of proportion, and some even use different perspectives. For someone who draws a lot, my proportions are always off. Many times the heads of the animals are drawn too big, while the legs are always too small.

After each child completes a drawing, he or she asks me to guess the name of the object. I often guess the incorrect answer just to make them feel comfortable with me. For example, I say that the picture of a *kujur* (spear) is a *peci* (cap).

They then exclaim, *"Bukon, nioma kujur!"* "You're wrong!! That's a spear!" Then a child runs to get a *kujur* and show it to me. I pretend to be oblivious, *"Ah kalu nioma apo? Peci?"* "Ah, what's this then? A cap?" My cluelessness irks them, *"Taun . . . kujur!"* "Oh no . . . it's a spear!" It is not inappropriate for them to think that they are teaching me about different objects, because I actually learn many things from them. Upon meeting his father, one child proudly says, *"Bepak, akeh lah mori Bontet polajoron!"* "Dad, I have just given Butet a lesson."

Every time I meet the children, I purposely make small mistakes. Being too optimistic, I ask, "Do you want to come to school with me?" They shake their heads to say no, and continue playing. They ignore me. Ooooh, how I regret asking that question. All of a sudden I feel so distant from them. How can I be so stupid? This is exactly how an inexperienced anthropologist would behave.

October 28, 1999
Would you like some rat?

It is late at night and I am fast asleep in a romantic dream, when *Indok* Terenong's scream startles me.

What in the world? What is wrong with these people? My dream with my Prince Charming dissipates . . .

I get up and look. Oh, it's just a rat. I go back to sleep. I saw the trap they set in the afternoon to catch this rat. It is interesting that they use the same mousetrap as the villagers. It is a simple iron wire cage with bait hanging inside. They say that they buy the traps at the market because they are portable and easy to use.

"*Bontet, tejegolah!*" "Butet, wake up!" *Indok* Terenong shouts.

They say that if I want to learn about the lives of the Orang Rimba I have to learn everything, including how to catch a jungle rat and how to cook it. Looking down to avoid eye contact, I grumble to myself. What? Rat? Yuck!! This is so disgusting. *Indok* holds the rat right in front of my face. "There goes my Prince Charming," I whisper to myself.

"*Koli guding, lomok nian tikuy niyo ma, beyik.*" "Look friend, this rat is fat, it's delicious." I shudder with dread. The rat is about 30 centimeters away from my nose. Why is it so cute? Is this really a rat? Why is his fur so thick and grey? Could it be a rabbit? *Indok* proudly tells me all about the rat while plucking its fur. The fur floats through the air like cotton. That rat is still alive! *Astaga!* He is still squeaking! I ask *Indok*, "Why don't you kill it before you skin it?" She replies, "*Ay, samo bae guding, todo sudah nivo, juga nye dibunuh.*" "Ah, it's all the same my friend, the rat's going to die anyway." It's true . . . but . . .

"*Mikay ndok cubo guding?*" "Would you like to try, my friend?" I refuse. I remember the sewer rats in Jakarta. But, this one is quite cute; he even resembles Mickey Mouse! Regardless, he is still a rat to me.

I curiously ask how she plans to cook the rat; it seems a bit small for a family meal. "What about Rantai and Ngali? Will they get a share?" She answers that they are not allowed to eat rat because it is taboo for girls. Here's my chance!

I exclaim, "*Akeh kan lah menjedi Orang Rimba, akeh menurut pula hopi bemakon tikuy mumpa budak lapay siyoh.*" "Well, I'm already like an Orang Rimba. So I will obey the rules and not eat rat like the girls here." *Indok* laughs and expresses how delighted she is that I am following the customs of the Orang Rimba. Phew, thank God I got away with that one.

October 29, 1999
Home again

Today is my last day in the rainforest before returning to the city. Even though Bangko is not as crowded as many of the cities on Java, I find the noise quite jarring. Ironically, when I first arrived from Jakarta, I felt that Bangko was as quiet as a deserted Boy Scout camp. Only a few buses and trucks pass by on the Lintas Sumatra Highway that divides the city into two.

Tijok picks me up on his motorbike. We ride along the motorbike trail. We fall into the mud and I laugh at the experience. I imagine that one day, I too will be able to drive a motorbike. The motorbike is an awesome vehicle; it makes me feel powerful just riding it.

My WARSI colleagues have been waiting for me at the office. When I enter, they gather around me, asking me questions and closely scrutinizing me. Now I understand that there aren't many people willing to work like this. This first visit becomes my benchmark. I could have just packed my bags and left, unwilling to work there anymore. But I have proved that I can survive. By now, I am crazy in love with life in the jungle.

Chapter 2

How does one begin?

November 15, 1999
Rombong Terap

On this trip, I visit a different *rombong*, located near the Terap River. According to WARSI policy I need to work with all the Orang Rimba, not just with those from one *rombong*. I arrive with my colleagues, Robert Aritonang and Diki Kurniawan. They have already developed a close relationship with this *rombong*. They help me to establish and introduce myself.

Rombong Terap is normally made up of 28 *pesaken*. However, when we arrive, there are only around half this number. Among them are *Depati* Mulung, *Menti* Maritua, *Mangku* Jujumbai, *Temenggung* Mija and *Wakil* Nyenong. The rest of the *rombong* is away paying their respects on a *melangun* trip to DAS Sakolado because *Temenggung's* stepmother has died.

One Orang Rimba man helps us set up a simple hut made with *gelogoh*, with a plastic sheet for a roof. The hut is located just next to the river. The Terap River is very clean, and wide, around 6 meters at this site. The surface of the water is around a meter lower than the riverbank, so we make a simple ladder to go down to the river.

Setting up camp is my favorite activity. I design the kitchen next to our hut; stick a branch in the ground to hang up all our plastic cups and plastic bags filled with spoons, salt, chili and other little things. It makes the cutest Christmas tree I have ever seen. Then, I make a simple table with four short poles, each ending in a fork. I place sticks between the forks along both sides, and then lay many small branches across the sticks—table done! How simple and cheap . . . in fact, it is free!!

November 16, 1999
First the flood, then the bee stings

This second day of this trip turns out to be the unforgettable one. I do not even write in my journal this day because I am so sick.

I wake up around nine in the morning. We are so tired from our nine-hour journey of the previous day that we sleep like logs. A sound wakes me—"ting . . . ting . . ."—like metal hitting metal. I open my eyes, no, only one eye, indolently, to look for the sound. I suddenly cry out, "Diki, Robert, wake up!! We're caught in a flood!!" They get up and join me in my panic.

I hear giggling and I look up. Damn! Those Orang Rimba are just crowding around and laughing at us. They are four meters away, further up the hill. They think this is very funny. "Huh, I have to agree with them," I tell myself.

I cannot believe it. We are surrounded by water and just three centimeters of air remained between the water and our hut floor. We built the floor one meter above the ground, and the river surface was one meter below bank, so there was a two-meter increase in one rainy night!

I see pots and pans floating into each other, making that metallic sound. Diki's shoes float past. "Hurry, you'll kill the fish with your stinky shoes!" I point them out. He grins and swims to save them. Robert and I try to save everything and move it to a higher level. We can't tell how much we have saved and how much has already sunk.

I start to make a fire under a big tree to prepare a late breakfast. Robert and Diki sort through our things, trying to dry out what remains in our wet backpacks. Luckily, our clothes were packed in plastic bags, but our foodstuff is soaked. Then, out of the blue, a bee stings me. The first one gets me on the nape of my neck and then another one stings my hand. I slap at it and try to kill it when another stings me. Again and again, I feel the stings and I hear Robert groaning. Together with the Orang Rimba around us, we look up into the tree. Hundreds of bees fly angrily to attack us.

The Orang Rimba suggest that I jump into the river while they run away, running back to protect their children from the bees' attack. I do not think twice. The stings, they are so painful they scare me. I run and run, and with a leap, dive into the river. In a few seconds, I hear Robert join me. I keep my head under water. Funny thing, my sarong floats up like a bubble. Later, Diki tells me that my sarong looked like a colorful jellyfish. I don't even try to pull my sarong down while I fight to keep my head under water. I hear the crowd laughing at me. I guess I have succeeded in entertaining them today.

Within a minute or so, I cannot breathe. I feel my eyelids swelling. I am in a panic, as I cannot continue to hold my breath, but I am too scared to raise my head; I am afraid of the bees. Before I run out of oxygen, Robert takes my hand. "You need to breathe above water, or you'll die!" So we breathe, over and over, for almost an hour and a half. The bees are still flying around the surface and every time we lift our heads they sting us. I keep glancing at Diki, why is he safe over there? I wonder. He is laughing at us while cleaning the camp and drying out our stuff. Diki had shown me his ring the other day; it was made from elephant tusk. "It's a magic ring, it prevents bee stings," he said.

The bees leave, but Robert and I remain alert, waiting for several long minutes. Robert thinks it is safe to climb out, so he gets out of the river. They try to convince me that the area is clear of bees, but I stay at the river's edge, hanging onto the ladder, with only my head out of the water. If the bee kingdom returns, I can easily dive back in. After another hour, I give up. By now, I am trembling from hunger and cold. My fingers are wrinkled. Everyone tells me to quickly change my clothes so the bees won't recognize me.

I run into the bush to get changed. What a relief to put on dry clothes and be free from those damn *rapah*. I am just about finished dressing, putting my foot into pants, when I hear the humming sound. What??? They are at it again! Bees fly into me. I scream, "Dikiii! Robert! They are stinging me again! Help, help, help!" I run while pulling up my pants. Robert hears me; he is hanging a mosquito net. Before he has a chance to hang the fourth corner, I arrive, followed by those fanatical bees, of course. Robert quickly goes inside the net and I jump in too. I hold onto the fourth corner with my hand to close the net. A few bees follow me in. We fight them inside the net, killing them wildly. The bees are still very angry; they keep trying to sting us. Some of them sting me through the mosquito netting. We look over at Diki as he continues cooking without a problem. Chuckling happily, he rubs his ring "What a magic ring!"

It is getting dark and the bees finally gone. My hands are stiff and my body aches all over. Oohh . . . enough! Enough, you bee gangsters, you win! This day is only about you! I have maybe fifty stings all over my body; I can't count them all. Soon I feel dizzy and a bit feverish. I still cannot understand why those bees were so angry with me.

Apparently, I had tried to cook under the tree where they keep their hives. They saw Robert cooking too. And Diki, he also cooked, but well,

I cannot explain in a scientific way why he was not stung. That night, I become a patient; I take paracetamol and finally fall into a peaceful sleep.

November 21, 1999
It's not easy being a teacher

A week has already gone by. I experience several fantastic moments. There is a memorable moment where I first take my pen out of my bag and the Rimba run away. They ask me to put the pen back in the bag, so they can come close again. They say a pen is "evil with spiky eyes"—very clever name.

Although I have established communications, I am reluctant to approach them further. They too keep their distance. I begin to wonder how my visit will conclude at the end of the month.

Robert and Diki have been asked to deliver a letter of authorization from the Forestry Department. It effectively grants the Orang Rimba authority to safeguard the rainforest. This includes the power to drive out any intruders found to be exploiting or logging the rainforest. One day, we walk for about two hours from the Terap River to the location of the *melangun*. Apparently the *Temenggung* has combined the *melangun* ceremony with the honey harvest. We deliver the letter to the *Temenggung* and his *Wakil* and explain its contents.

The five women from *rombong* Terap not participating in the *melangun* are quite close to me. They are *Indok* Betayam, *Indok* Besbin, *Indok* Mentaro (wife of Ngelemboh), *Indok* Kirah and Meti's wife. Despite our closeness, our interaction is limited and confined to reciprocal visits, communal bathing and casual conversations while attending to the medical needs of some of the girls suffering severely from boils.

The women ask a lot of questions about life in the city, or as they call it, the *Dunia Orang Terang* (world of people in the open and light). They have many personal questions such as *"Calon laki Bontet kinilah semendo di mono?"* (Where does your fiancé live?) Or, pointing to my male colleagues, *"Nang mono laki kawan?"* (Which one is your husband?)

I find the task of explaining life in the outside world quite complicated because it differs so much from the realities of their daily life and from their cultural framework of thinking. On top of that, my limited Rimba vocabulary makes the task even more difficult. As much as I attempt to explain, the ideas seem to be beyond their grasp. They become further perplexed when I express my intention to make solo visits in the future. They are completely dumfounded by the idea of a woman travelling on her own and find it quite extraordinary.

Throughout my interactions with the Orang Rimba, I am constantly on the lookout for potential pupils to participate in our education program. I find three promising adult candidates. They are *Depati* Mulung (29 years old), *Menti* Maritua (43 years old), and Menyurau (25 years old). I am guessing their ages. Younger pupils are easy to find, perhaps because it is easier to interact with the children. In general, they are communicative, friendly, playful and very helpful.

It occurs to me that starting off my program with children might be a more effective strategy. The only hurdle is that out of the twenty potential youngsters, aged four to sixteen, most are male. The female students include Besilam (4 years old), Betuyah (5 years old), Betayam (4-5 years old) and Mangku (10 years old). It is very difficult to approach the girls, even by the end of my visit.

I have the impression that the women and girls have been taught to be cautious of outsiders, making them more difficult to reach. The fact that I arrived with men may have posed another problem. An instance of this caution comes up during bathing when some young girls cry out in fear when I offer some soap. The older girls reject it outright, pretending not to care. On the other hand, the boys accept it happily and use it to their hearts' content.

I begin to notice that during meals, the women sit behind the men. This signals to me that I should do the same and join them at the back. I also feel that there is an unwritten law that prohibits females from teaching, be it males or females. I know at least that it is considered *"hopi beik"* (out of place) for the men to be taught by a woman. On the other hand, the women may just be disinterested and, to some extent, a little fearful.

Interestingly, when I ask four boys to participate in the program, they express a desire to learn how to write and draw. They cover their wooden hut walls with black chalk drawings and attempts at the alphabet. However, when we meet together with other children and two older men, called Lidapenado and Ngelemboh, they change their minds. They simultaneously respond, *"hopi"* (no) when asked by Robert whether they want to learn how to read and write. The main reason given for the boy's reaction is that "it is not a part of our culture".

I feel betrayed. At the same time, I sense it is too risky to pursue the issue, and thus refrain from pressing the matter. Maybe it is our approach. Perhaps the concept of learning should be seen in a broader perspective, with a variety of different cultural settings or patterns of delivery. I do not know what form it should take, but one thing is clear. This program with the children has proven to be ineffective.

November 23, 1999
City Visit

The four of us, Robert, Diki, *Depati* Mulung and I depart at 11 o'clock for the district capital of Sarolangun. We are accompanying *Depati* Mulung because he wants to sell his produce and purchase provisions. After trekking on foot for half an hour, we arrive at our motorcycle "hide out" deep in a thicket at the periphery of the rainforest. We continue to travel by motorcycle on dirt roads of loose red earth. It takes us six hours to cover eighty kilometers. We stop for the night at a colleague's office.

November 24, 1999
Pay One by One

Today we go to Sarolangun market. Here, I find that the price of honey ranges from Rp. 12,000 to 15,000 per kilogram, while at Yatim's kiosk, which is a two-hour trek from *Depati* Mulung's *rombong,* it costs only Rp 3,000 per kilogram. I realize that the Orang Rimba's lack of information about the outside world places them at a gross disadvantage. Outsiders consider their community a soft target. This fact motivates me further to bring education to them, particularly for market trading.

Interactions between the Orang Rimba and the villagers are filled with suspicion and are often very troublesome. During transactions, you can clearly see how the Orang Rimba remain suspicious of outsiders. *Depati* Mulung, speaking in a basic form of *Melayu,* pays for each item individually rather than collectively.

Depati Mulung tells me he does this because he is afraid of being cheated. The stall owner is equally irritated by this manner of conducting business.

Depati Mulung begins by asking *"Berapo gula sekilu?"* (How much is a kilo of sugar?) *"Tiga ribu!"* (Three thousand!), the vendor replies.

Depati Mulung immediately responds, *"Minta sekilu, balikkan tujuh belas ribu!"* (Give me a kilogram of sugar and return seventeen thousand!) while handing over a Rp. 20,000 note.

As soon as he receives the change, he asks right away, *"Tembeko Kerinci berapo?* (How much for Kerinci brand tobacco?) *"Enam ribu!"*

(Six Thousand!) the vendor answers. He then hands over the stack of rupiah notes totaling Rp. 17,000 and says, *"Balikkan sebelas ribu!"* (Return eleven thousand to me!)

"Beras berapo?" (How much for uncooked rice?). *"Dua ribu!"* (Two thousand!) *"Mintak 5 kilu!"* (Give me five kilograms!) He says while offering more money and requesting change.

Now bear in mind that the money returned from the previous purchase is more than enough to cover the cost of the next purchase. Transactions continue in this manner.

Speaking in Indonesian, the owner of the stall says to me, "This is how it goes *Mbak*, when the Orang Rimba shop. They do not want to do it all at once, which gives me a headache. If there are more than twenty Orang Rimba buyers it makes things very frustrating."

I just smile. *Depati* adds that if he does not do it this way the vendor will cheat him. I smile again and say, "What if the price of rice is Rp. 1,750 and you want to buy fifteen kilos? Does he still have to return the money each time for each kilo?" *Depati* thinks for a moment and answers firmly, *"Au lah!"* (Yes, of course!)

December 2, 1999
The meaning of progress

The idea of progress is often measured within the context of modernity; big cosmopolitan cities such as Jambi and Jakarta symbolize progress. When the Central Forestry Department from Jakarta visits us to survey the expansion of the Bukit Dua Belas Biosphere Reserve, it is evident how the foresters understand the word "development". To our disappointment, they condemn WARSI on the basis that we have somehow isolated the Orang Rimba to keep them "backward" and make them objects of tourism. This can only mean that, either they do not quite comprehend our real objective or that they already have preconceived notions about it.

The Forestry Department's plans for development in the Reserve are based on their operations on Java. They assume that the living conditions of the Orang Rimba are due to poverty and ignorance. In reality, the Orang Rimba are neither poor nor ignorant. Have the foresters considered how they appear to the Orang Rimba? From the Orang Rimba's perspective, the *Orang Terang* (people from outside the rainforest) often look foolish in the middle of the rainforest and are ridiculed by the Orang Rimba.

This same 'modern' idea of development is reflected in the Forestry Department's proposal to boost bee farming and rattan production for the benefit of the Orang Rimba. The reason for this economic intervention is not explained and it confuses the Orang Rimba who neither need nor want the intervention.

It becomes clear that the Orang Rimba are not fully informed about what the outside world can offer. In some circumstances, it is simply that the intervention programs are not practical. Other reasons are debated over the course of long discussions dominated by officials. We hold back voicing our opinions out of respect for the Orang Rimba who are there with us. We also do this because as employees of WARSI our focus is on other programs. Through the course of the debates, the Forestry officials act as if they are superior and fully understand the situation. We find we are given little opportunity to advocate another position. What is the point of this argument if it does not take into account the point of view of the Orang Rimba?

In the end, we develop the view that the most important objective is to expand the tropical rainforest reserve. With this end in mind, we are able to disregard their opinions on development. It amuses me when Robert comments to one of the Orang Rimba men while shaking hands with a representative from the Forestry Department, "Sir, you are aware of the situation right? This gentleman is going to help to expand the rainforest reserve, so please don't put a hex on him."

The Forestry Department officials are shocked. I hear later, from the driver, that none of the officials dared to spit out of the window during their journey back to Jambi. They either spat into tissues or their handkerchiefs for fear of being cursed. (In Indonesia, it is commonly believed that rainforest tribes have powerful magic and that in this case, one can be cursed using one's own spit!)

December 5, 1999
Inspiring Helen

Today, I meet with Professor Helen Cruz of the World Bank. She plans to visit the Orang Rimba a day after I leave the jungle. We discuss the concept of "backwardness" which were the focal point of discussions with the Forestry Department officials and staff. She strongly challenges their way of thinking. Helen has studied a great deal about the life of the Orang Rimba She knows that the culture of the Orang Rimba is essentially oriented toward nature and they are more environmentally sound and aware than their city counterparts.

In this context, the city folk are "backward". City people use the river for all their activities, causing pollution. Conversely, the rainforest tribes understand that disease originates upstream. Their beliefs stem from animism, where they are taught to prioritize the preservation of nature and peace. We also talk about how the Orang Rimba, though not formally educated, are capable of protecting themselves against diseases and external influences.

Helen gives the example of the Native Americans in Canada who were able to re-claim their land successfully. Their victory might encourage the Orang Rimba to be more vocal about their struggle. In my opinion, however, there is a substantial difference between the Indonesian community, particularly in Jambi, and the Canadians, who are more respectful of indigenous communities.

The following day Professor Cruz drops by our office again. She tells us about her meeting with the government officials to discuss the Orang Rimba. In her opinion, the discussion was very disturbing because it was clear that the officials held the Orang Rimba in low regard. This was reflected in their derogatory manner and their unsympathetic laughter when discussing issues concerning the Orang Rimba. They described how smelly, naked and stupid these primitive *Kubu* people are. She says, "This is not at all funny."

Their use of the term *kubu* in particular demonstrates that they have no respect for the Orang Rimba. *Kubu* is a Malay term meaning primitive or wild and connoting someone or something dirty, perhaps difficult or even stupid. Unfortunately, the first foreign researchers to this area used the term *"Orang Kubu"* in academic papers about the Orang Rimba, because that is what they heard people outside the rainforest calling them. These researchers did not know what the word meant or that the Rimba never referred to themselves in this way.

In retrospect, the opinions of the city people do not make any sense to my peers at WARSI or to me. In our view, the Orang Rimba are not primitives to be looked down on.

I remain convinced that education is a constructive step forward for the Orang Rimba. Education can be a tool of empowerment to fend off aggressive threats from the outside world. Of course, not everyone who becomes literate ends up being a doctor, engineer or a community leader. But neither is it possible to be a doctor, engineer or community leader without first being literate. Maybe at this time, the Orang Rimba do not yet see education as essential.

Education does not just mean being literate and mathematically adept. Education enables people to increase their standard of living and can give the Orang Rimba an understanding of their rights in their own jungle. Only then can they determine their way of life in the context of the outside world and have the freedom to choose the development path for their future. Where do we begin? It is already so difficult to approach them.

I have to calm down. I realize that under these circumstances, good intentions are not enough. Likewise, I still have no notion of the type or form of education that would best suit them. I am troubled by a niggling thought, "Do they really need it?"

I am still not quite sure of my own convictions. There is plenty more to learn and understand.

Chapter 3

Do not meddle in our traditions

February 2, 2000
Where to next?

In February, I am able to spend seventeen days in the jungle. I choose between two *rombong,* one near the Bernai River and the other near the Tengkuyungon River. The first *rombong* is located in the north and the other is a two-day trek to the south of Bukit Dua Belas National Park. Both locations are hard to reach and I need to summon all my courage to withstand the feeling of disgust caused by blood-sucking leeches latching onto my legs. I am accompanied by Hadi, a surveyor conducting an Orang Rimba population census, which includes mapping their locations. Bintoro, a geographer, and Willy, another surveyor, are traveling in the same direction. They pass us on their way to their destination, which is a further three-hour trek into the jungle.

Actually, when I visited the rainforest last December, I thought that I would go to the Tengkuyungon River but now I am not so sure. I am interested in exploring the interior of the Bukit Dua Belas National Park. Perhaps there is a better location? The *rombong* I visited last month at Tengkuyungon housed the WARSI learning program managed by former WARSI education facilitator, Yusak. He died from malaria recently, after working for 10 months and almost succeeding in starting the education program. I went there to continue his attempt to bring education to the Orang Rimba. Another two education facilitators joined this project, and failed after working on it for a year. Yusak's style was a bit different from mine.

I decide I will start afresh with students who request an education rather than bargaining and trying to convince them.

February 3, 2000
Rombong Belambun Pupus

The Bernai River location was initially suggested by the program coordinator and a colleague from the WARSI research unit. Based on my understanding of the discussions, WARSI uses three main criteria to select areas for community education for the Orang Rimba. First and most important is ease of access. Second, the degree of permanence of the settlement is a factor. Third, a sufficient number of potential students have to be identified before an education facilitator is directed to an area.

The criteria confuse me. Why did they choose these three? In my opinion, the further we venture into the rainforest the more fascinating and challenging it becomes. WARSI also concluded that, if we are stationed at accessible locations, it is easier for governors or influential people to visit us. Presumably first hand knowledge of these programs increases their support of WARSI programs. Is this truly the case? I am puzzled.

The *rombong* I head towards is located along the Belambun Pupus River, a tributary of the Bernai River in the north of Bukit Dua Belas National Park. The leader of this *rombong* is *Wakil* Tuha, better known by the outside community as *Datuk*. He is the deputy of *Temenggung* Makekal Hilir, also known as *Temenggung* Bedinding Besi. The community consists of twelve families, a total of forty-nine people. They live in four locations within a five to fifteen minute walk from each other. We reach the first *rombong* group after walking for an hour from the last village community called *TSM* or Swakarsa Mandiri Transmigration Unit A. Once there, under *Wakil* Tuha's jurisdiction, we build a temporary hut. This *rombong* group relocated here four months ago after the *melangun* for the death of *Indok* Sekodi's child, the grandson of *Wakil* Tuha.

February 4, 2000
The wrong approach

As I prepare dinner for the four of us at seven in the evening, we strike up a conversation with *Wakil* Tuha, his wife, and three *Bepak*. To my surprise, Willy and Hadi, the two surveyors (who I playfully called Fido Dido or Thomson and Thompson because of their odd combination of silliness, recklessness and kind-heartedness), announce formally that my mission here is to teach the local population reading and writing. Adding, *"Mae kawana hopi lolo lagi"* (So that you Orang Rimba won't be stupid anymore.) Bintoro just smiles at me.

I trust that this approach is appropriate since Willy and Hadi know the Orang Rimba best. But, the reaction they get is totally unexpected. Our intentions are completely rejected. Several of the adult tribesmen shout uncontrollably; they are obviously infuriated. I begin to shiver with fear.

Bintoro gives me a detailed explanation of what is going on. He says that the Orang Rimba despise being called stupid and because we explicitly told them that we brought "education" with us, the tribesmen are afraid that my arrival will bring bad luck. They also think that education will spoil and damage their traditional culture. A pen, for example, is associated with the cheating outsiders at the markets. Bintoro then says that the Orang Rimba request that I leave immediately because they do not want any form of schooling.

Meanwhile, Willy and Hadi continue to argue with them to try to convince them of the benefits of our proposal. When my colleagues ask me to join the conversation, I can only add that education is useful to prevent the Orang Rimba from being cheated by the outsiders, the *Orang Terang*. They remain unmoved, and say, "If they cheat us, then let God judge them! *Jengon mikay usik-usik adat kami!"* (Do not meddle in our traditions!)

Oh, I feel terrible. What they said echoes day and night in my thoughts—do not meddle in our traditions! Deep down in my heart I am in conflict. How can tradition be respected? How can the Orang Rimba protect themselves from exploitation from outsiders? Are my good intentions in reality damaging their culture and their future?

February 6, 2000
I sadly say goodbye

The dark days following that eventful evening were filled with suspicion. I tried to approach the Orang Rimba again, just to ease the tension. I did not dare to have even a glimmer of hope that my education mission would continue here.

In time, they start to accept me, although not openly. Slowly, unintended familiarity creeps in and communication follows. During this tense period, they recount stories of how many times they have gone on *melangun* journeys and the various reasons for them. They generously give me gifts of seasonal fruit such as durian, *duku,* rambutan, *dekat*, jackfruit, *kemang* and *tampoy*. They even allow me to accompany them into the rainforest to gather fruit.

One time, when I was having difficulty finding a sleeping mat for the hut I was making, *Wakil* Tuha graciously helped me out. Hadi prefers to use the tent that we brought from Bangko. He offers it to me first, but I dislike sleeping in tents here. For me, tents are suitable for use on mountain hikes or for those who are only staying in a place for a short period. Sleeping in a tent for days in the middle of the jungle, especially in the midst of an Orang Rimba *rombong*, seems a bit odd. For them, a tent is novel and strange.

They are also bemused to see me eat wild boar meat and other game they bring back from the rainforest. It never occurs to them that outsiders are willing to eat animals commonly forbidden in Islamic culture in the "other world". They think that outsiders are all Muslims who do not eat pork and that city people do not eat game. Apparently, my eating habits cause a sensation and the news is passed on to newly arrived Orang Rimba.

The Orang Rimba have difficulty pronouncing "Butet", so they change my name to "Bontet", just as they had at *rombong* Tengkuyungon. Eventually, in recognition of my courage for eating wild boar, I am nicknamed "Bontet *nangoy*" or Bontet, the brave or the rebellious to denote that I am either brave or rebellious enough to go against my faith! I really had no intention of eating anything generally regarded as taboo. However, I am a Christian who can eat pork and I am unfortunately one of those indiscriminate people, seldom noticing the difference in flavors of various meats. Consuming this meat is not just necessary for survival; it is also part of my strategy for assimilating into the Orang Rimba community. If they regard a particular item as food, I happily scoff it down with them.

I thoroughly enjoy my stay at the *rombong* Bernai. I have access to an abundance of meat, root vegetables, reasonably clear spring water, and am spoiled with the selection of fruit. I even suffer bouts of diarrhea from eating too much durian. *Wakil* Tuha, Hadi and I once devoured nine durians at one go. I thought to myself, "Wow. How much would this have cost in Jakarta?" And it wouldn't have tasted as good either!

In reality, it is not just the food that makes my stay enjoyable with this *rombong*. I find it intriguing to meet people who steadfastly hold on to their culture and the traditional laws inherited from their ancestors. I sincerely admire and support them, even when my colleagues at WARSI perceive them to be a closed culture, highly bound by tradition.

It is true that all Orang Rimba strongly observe their traditions. They are a people who still live like hunter-gatherers and are dependent upon the resources of the rainforest directly as opposed to those who cultivate their land. For the Orang Rimba, nature's gift of sustenance is the ultimate contentment.

This adherence to their customs is what makes *rombong Wakil Tuha* hold on so strongly to their way of life despite the fact that their habitat is only a two-hour trek from the nearest migrant community. In addition to the proximity of the migrant community, there are other intrusions. Palm oil plantations and areas of dry-bed rice cultivation surround their settlement. Loggers camp close to the *rombong*. The Orang Rimba now live among rubber plantations that are tapped once or twice a week.

The strong adherence to tradition makes it difficult for the Orang Rimba to accept the idea of receiving an education. Even though WARSI has thought through their program guidelines and their three criteria, an additional criterion—open to the idea of the importance of literacy—should have been included. It is unfortunate that the program will not be accepted by this *rombong* because there are many children who are about nine years old, who have the same potential to learn as children in Tengkuyungon. At this young age, they are too naïve to appreciate the significance of education in their lives. To me, it is the most promising age to start an education.

There were instances when I became too friendly with people in the group, especially *Wakil* Tuha's wife, *Indok* Sekodi and *Indok* Nyado. They are mindful about keeping their distance; this prompts the occasional question, "When are you going home?" or simply, "Go home!" There is a similar reaction when Hadi and I visit each *sudung* gathering to map out their exact coordinates by GPS.

It is quite obvious that they feel uneasy and dislike our arrival. One woman says, quite directly, "Go home and do not come back again." Another says, "My child is ill, you brought the disease!" I then realize that as long as I am associated with the outside world and bringing education, they will always be suspicious.

That first night's outburst left a deep impression on their minds. I sadly say a good-bye in my heart. It is not good to impose on people, even with the best of intentions. Education for the Orang Rimba should only be offered when they feel the need for it.

February 8, 2000
False destination

Not long before our departure, two tribesmen Nyereban (19 years old) and Kedilam (17 years old) from *rombong Bepak* Melurai on the Kemang River drop by on their return from a day trip to the market at the Tanagaro Transmigration Unit. One of them is sporting a watch worn backwards. He doesn't know how to read it, so we teach him. It is a difficult exercise to explain the concept of time in minutes and seconds. I have never had to teach this to anyone before. While we are discussing reading numbers, they mention that the issue of education was raised during the gathering at Bangko with their clan leader, *Bepak* Melurai, and our colleague, Agus.

"*Bepak* Agus promised to send us someone to teach us reading and writing. We have been waiting for this for a long time." These comments from the two young men give me great hope. They add thoughtfully, "Reading and writing will not change our religion and traditions, but it will help us in our work."

Nyereban and Kedilam are very excited when they recount their work in the rubber plantation. They express a desire to be able to write their names, to weigh the rubber and to count the money earned from their hard labor. They are convinced that outsiders often cheat them by underestimating the total weight of their rubber but they can never prove this.

The two of them notice the discrepancy by the irregular amount of money they receive. For example, the total weight of their most recent sale seemed twice as heavy as the previous sale, but the money they received was just marginally more. They want to master the basic mathematics needed for their job so that they can avoid being cheated.

"*Akeh koli, nye pakoy mesin hitung, Ibu. Akeh endok ngitung juga, tapi hopi tentu angko-angko berapo yoya.*" (I saw him using a calculator, *Ibu*. I would also like to do my own calculations, but I don't understand the numbers that appear on the machine.)

They even discuss arranging their work schedule to fit in time for study at mid-day or in the afternoon. The Orang Rimba usually tap rubber trees in the morning and return home at noon for lunch. After that, they return to the rubber plantation and finish work at around four. From this conversation, I conclude that those most interested in learning are young men who work as tappers at the rubber plantation. I express my concern about resistance from the Orang Rimba elders, but they tell me not to worry. *Bepak* Melurai will take care of everything because there are many tappers who want to study.

They even offer to build a sturdy *susudungon* and ask for my preferred style and size of hut. They make me promise I will come to their camp, so they can expect a lesson. I am ready to agree immediately, when Hadi reminds me that at WARSI one cannot act alone. I cannot re-assign myself to a different area or an Orang Rimba site on my own authority. I sigh in my heart. Oh, if only I had the autonomy to make my own plans. I am the person working in the field, so I am the best person to know what is right for me to do next. At least give me a walkie-talkie or a satellite phone or an Internet connection, so I can ask for approval immediately. In the end, I can only promise I will try my best to return to them as soon as possible.

I wonder about the degree of difficulty associated with access to their *rombong* along the Kemang River. According to Hadi, there is a shortcut through *rombong* Bedinding Besi, about an hour from the rainforest's edge and through the transmigrants' palm oil plantation. From there on, the encampment is only about a ninety-minute trek into the interior of the jungle. It really isn't a short distance. My exact destination is the Makekal tributary of the Kemang River in the Pekasang Pematong Derumbai village. There are 12 *pesaken* living there.

I suddenly realize how disastrous it could be if I land in the wrong *rombong*. What if my coordinator actually assigned me to the two Rimba *rombong* located at *Sungai* Kemang and not to the one here at *Sungai* Bernai? Ah, silly Butet, you've always lacked a sense a direction. If only you had written down the name of the *rombong*, it would have been much easier to find it. It is not enough to know the general area and that the rainforest is to the North or what the area downstream looks like. The jungle is huge!

Anyway, I cannot just move to the *rombong* of these two tribesmen. Only two days remain, not enough time to travel back and forth. I have to fulfill the work plan I made with WARSI during our workshop, and so I will visit another group in the South in the second half of the month.

February 9, 2000
I do not like villages

I spend the night in a village at the Tanagaro Transmigration Unit in the Pariyan's family home. The family regularly accommodates WARSI staff on their way to the Makekal Hilir *rombong*. The houses here are quite austere. They have earthen floors and use oil lamps for light. So, at night, the ambience is similar to that of the rainforest. The only difference is that here we have walls, as well as a wooden chair and a table. Now, I find sitting around in this confined space cramped and claustrophobic. There is little privacy. We gather together in the same room and make empty, courteous conversations with the family the entire night, until sleep takes over.

Another difference in the village is that I have to fetch water from the well using a pail. For lazy people like me, it is easier to bathe in the river than to carry big buckets of water to the village. In the jungle, all you need to do is to take a dip in the river and let the current wash you clean.

There is another complication while staying in the village. I find that I have become more prone to diarrhea and have difficulty finding a lavatory. In the village, the residents make a sort of latrine using a wooden plank with a hole in the center. The diameter of the hole is just a little bit larger than the size of the poop. Ewwwwww!! It is disgusting. Just being near it makes me nauseous, especially when I see fat green flies hovering over the hole. Ah, not to mention the stench!! In the jungle, I just dig a new hole in the ground. There is always a fresh spot to choose.

On the bright side, *Ibu* Pariyan is from Pati, Central Java and she is always happy to massage my scalp when I lay my head on her lap. She also happily cooks my favorite fried *tempe* (fermented soya bean cake) or sweet and spicy omelets. I am spoiled. She does not allow me to help with the chores in the kitchen, saying I am too tired from working in the rainforest. On second thought, she might be afraid that I will mess up her kitchen or eat up everything!

February 10, 2000
Rombong Laman on the Tengkuyungon River

I arrive at *rombong* Laman with Hadi, but he has to leave me alone here to go to work in a different location. I then head towards *rombong* Tengkuyungon, which is about 75 minutes away, where they are buying honey and selling rubber sap. They are also guarding some timber, which has been cut by illegal loggers. The loggers have not as yet been able to collect the timber. By the time I arrive, the Rimba have been staying at this location for five days. They plan to stay for eleven days and head back to their dry-bed rice field in Tengkuyungon.

When I arrive this time, I see only Cangking, Laman, Lurah (Cangking's in-law) and Cerinay. Cerinay is now known as *Bepak* Maduguno, following Rimba naming conventions, because he has a newborn baby named Maduguno. Meanwhile, *Pesaken* Ngandun (*Bepak* Terenong) has left to work the paddy fields at Seranti in Pengelaworon. Grandma Ngampun and Resnah are also on their way there with the Orang Rimba from Gemuruh River. Terenong and Merendung are traveling into the outside world. So, in total, only seven *pesaken* potential students remain.

While in the *rombong*, I am always accompanied by Kembang, a very friendly girl who talks about everything. She is full of questions, and especially curious about the city. I make a point of answering her questions as completely as possible.

Meanwhile, *Indok* Kembang who stays in the hut next to me asks me directly what my real intentions are in coming back. *Bepak* Kembang, on the contrary, is always discreet. He guards and feeds me without question and shows no suspicion about my presence. On the other hand, Laman, the head of the *rombong*, is very cautious toward me, quite different from his wife who is friendly, open and good-humored.

Cerinay, Laman's brother, is his usual positive self; helpful and constructive toward all WARSI staff members. Thankfully the children's attitude has not changed much from my previous visit; they remain easy-going and friendly.

There are three children with whom I have continuous contact: Bekingkim, Belanka, and Gemurak. Other children like those of *Bepak* Terenong and Merendung aren't around for some reason. Kembang, whom I have never met before, immediately makes me a *sudung* out of the palm branches. She says that although she did not met me when I visited previously, she has heard stories about me from Rantai and Ngali, the daughters of *Bepak* Terenong, and so she really wanted to meet me.

Since my arrival, the other children quickly join in to tease me and joke with me. There are around fifteen kids, many of them are just toddlers, too young to go to school. They play and cry throughout the day.

February 11, 2000
A sudden change of attitude

Something strange is happening today. All the children are forbidden to approach me. If one of them gets too close, they are reprimanded. Kembang and Belanka, who had accompanied me the day before, also avoid me and I am not allowed to approach them. I am confused. What has caused this sudden change of attitude? What have I done?

They look at me with such disdain, almost with hatred. I try hard to think of a reason, but end up confused; I cannot think of anything. Nobody wants to answer me except *Indok* Kembang. She explains that *Bepak* Bekingkim had a dream. In his dream, he received a message—Bontet is carrying diseases that can't be seen. In a short time, all the diseases in her body will break loose and plague the people. So, Bontet must be *besasanding* (isolated). I feel so discouraged; I make plans to leave the very next day.

Oddly, the next day everyone is warm and friendly toward me, as if nothing has happened. I do not have a clue what is going on. Maybe it is because I do not get sick after all. At times like this I become livid, I feel like knocking their heads together.

In the days that follow, I go with them into the nearby rainforest to look for *gelogoh*, fruit and firewood. I fish in the local river and play around with the children. They seem to like me. We make funny faces, bathe together, run around the plantation, and even joke around passing gas at each other. It feels weird joking around while farting at each other. Here, passing gas is not thought to be an embarrassment; it is part of being human and a natural bodily function. Passing gas is certainly not considered impolite. I am happy that I have started to make friends.

If there is a naughty or lazy kid with us, the other children ask me not to talk to him or give him candy or cookies. Then, the child tries to be good and diligent. Their willingness to do chores like fetching water, starting a fire or bathing demonstrates their desire to be good. Sometimes I feel a bit cruel depriving them of a candy treat, but I keep quiet. I feel that at the moment, doing what the majority want is important, and besides, I have other plans for them. He he he . . . .

Near the end of my stay, Hadi comes to pick me up. In these final days, we stay at Cerinay's *sudung pesaken*. He is the only tribesman living in the jungle who can read and write moderately well and count a bit. He has ventured throughout the provinces of Jambi all the way to Palembang. Cerinay told us that he once returned with books to teach the local children how to read, color and count. But none of them were interested and the books eventually got ruined.

According to him, people in this *rombong* think that they only need to work hard, harvest the resources of the rainforest and sell them to the outside world for cash. They never want to live like the "people of light". They like their jungle existence and, while interested in making money from selling honey in order to buy cookies or radios, they don't see any advantage in being able to read or write. They fail to see the strong correlation between literacy and making money.

I make a note to remember his informative insights.

Chapter 4

If Only They Could Read

March 7, 2000
My new assignment

Here I am again, in the jungle, seemingly in the twilight of a mythical part of the world. I come lugging the same burden I had on my previous visits. I am the facilitator of education. I am here to recruit students come what may! They have to believe in me. Or sometimes I think that maybe I am here to recruit students by deceiving them and tricking them into an education.

I feel a bit pressured in front of my colleagues at WARSI because I know they are expecting me to recruit students quickly, although they do not say this out loud. I am to set the example for WARSI. I am to prove to the external world that the Orang Rimba can receive and benefit from education.

I can't help smiling to myself as it occurs to me that my work has a missionary aspect to it. Whatever their religious orientation, all missionaries strive to find new recruits to atone for their "deficiencies", as defined by their particular version of truth, and then to be reborn. I apologize for being so blunt, but in my experience, I know that some missionaries prefer quantity over quality when it comes to converts. As soon as a person declares conversion to the religion, they are immediately counted as a new member. I recall a conversation with one Orang Rimba that made quite an impression on me. He said, "I have converted to (a new) religion, *Ibu*. It is great. I have received presents such as rice, sugar, tobacco, and even clothes. Not to mention a cooking pot and some frying utensils . . . you name it!"

I promise myself I would never do such a thing, giving away gifts like that. It cheapens religion to use presents as bait. I do not want education to be that way. I would prefer that the Rimba fall in love with the idea of literacy, find value in reading and writing, and see the benefits to their lives. But then, how do I do this?

Alas, I am acting exactly like those officials with all their jargon who pretend to have altruistic motives. "We have to eradicate poverty, ineptitude and corruption. We must improve the morale of our citizens. Create an Indonesia that is prosperous! Increase the Indonesian people's welfare! Boost the nutrition of our mothers and children! Wipe out malaria, malnutrition, tuberculosis and AIDS!" In brief, the citizens are the top priority, right. But seriously, everybody knows about all that. The question is how do we do it? Like those preachers pontificating, "You have to pray all the time, be accepting, to be resilient in the face of trials and tribulations, to love mankind, to not steal, lie, kill, rape. Because if you don't, you will go straight to hell!"

As for me, I am probably just as clueless as those officials and preachers. I know my goal but I have no idea how to get there. There is no other way but to plunge into the deep end and figure out how to swim later. Surely, the ideas will come. The only problem is my fear of failure. It horrifies me to think that I will go back to Jakarta without having any students or Rimba friends.

I read the reports of the late Yusak as well as others who have been education facilitators at WARSI. I study the reasons why they all failed because I want to learn from their mistakes. I take note when they write about failing to gain student's trust or neglecting to develop successful relationships. Unfortunately they do not write directly about these matters. Most of the writing is either general or consists of program data. I do not learn much that I can apply to my work. Some reports are extremely theoretical or heavy on advocacy. Ah, I am too lazy and stupid to understand such things . . .

I am driven in the office car directly to the house of Pak Pariyan at the Tanagaro Transmigration Unit. My colleague Diki accompanies me, as well as Pak Zul, a villager who works as a guide for WARSI staff.

Diki is responsible for taking me to familiar destinations. During this field trip I plan to visit *rombong Temenggung* Bedinding Besi. I intend to visit the groups I have not met yet. The dispersed groups in this area all belong to a larger group associated with *Wakil* Tuha. My visit this month is a follow up to the request of the two tribesmen I met last month.

First, we visit the groups around the Bernai River, Sako Keranji River and Kemang River. The route along these rivers forms a corridor to the southwestern part of the rainforest. I also plan to take time to visit the main group of *Temenggung* Bedinding Besi. I have never met the *Temenggung* and am curious about him. What is he like? No doubt, he will be stern and skilled at magic rites, spells and sorcery. His name alone is unusual. Why Bedinding Besi ("steel wall")? Why not another more familiar type of wall like concrete or wood? He has other names as well—Bejumbai was his original name before he married and became a *temenggung*.

March 8, 2000
The Orang Rimba become ill

Temenggung Bedinding Besi leads a group of around 75 people. This group consists of 14 families living in five smaller groups. It takes about two-and-a-half hours by car from Bangko to reach this *rombong*, which is located near the periphery of the rainforest at Jeramba, also known as Bernai Bridge. The road between Bangko and Margoyoso (Transmigration Unit G) provides serviceable vehicular access, but the surface deteriorates severely when it rains, so the trip can stretch to over four hours.

Smaller groups are led by Nitip (*Bepak* Bepiun), Mesebah (*Bepak* Sejankang), Bejumbai (Bedinding Besi), Ngukir (*Bepak* Nangguk) and Ngagung (*Bepak* Megang). Their settlements are located within five minutes, ten minutes, half an hour, one hour and two hours respectively of the Jeramba Bernai Road.

When we arrive at the village of Tanagaro Transmigration Unit, we receive a report that the *rombong* of the *Temenggung* left three days before to perform *melangun*.

The grandchild of the *Temenggung* has died. The Rimba have gone to the Tanagaro Transmigration Unit's palm oil plantation for *melangun*. Even though not all tribal leaders participate in this *melangun*, as the days pass an increasing number of Orang Rimba arrive to join in. As the *melangun* progresses, people start falling ill. It is evident that there is some sort of disease spreading among the Orang Rimba. Eventually nearly all of the Orang Rimba here become infected. Most of them suffer from fever, cough and flu-like symptoms. Their health worsens gradually.

Although they have been here for four days, not one of them is willing to accompany us to the home of the tribal chief, *Bepak* Melurai, on the banks of the Kemang River. To prevent the spread of disease it is strictly forbidden to visit other Orang Rimba groups once someone falls ill. It is incredible that they know which diseases require isolation and which do not. They know that headaches, inflamed livers (from acute malaria) and muscle injuries are not contagious. On the other hand, they know that sufferers of coughs, flu, malaria, and all sorts of skin diseases must be *besasanding* or isolated.

Disease is part of the Orang Rimba's life. They have no vaccinations and little medicine, so diseases spread easily. Just imagine, if one *rombong* is plagued by a cough, the whole jungle experiences a coughing festival.

March 12, 2000
Family names

We settle into a deserted illegal loggers' camp nearby. This place is considered to be an Orang Rimba *bungaron*, a place for people who are healthy and unlikely to fall sick. The *pesaken* had six members: *Bepak* Sejangkang and *Indok* Sejangkang, and their four sons, Sejangkang (15), Begunung (13), Betingkar (7), and Besunting (5).

The name *Bepak* Sejangkang signifies that his first child is named Sejangkang. I am still intrigued that the Orang Rimba's naming convention is exactly the same as the *Batak* custom. This reminds me of my family. My name is Saur and I am the first child in my family. My late father was called *Ama* Saur, literally the father of Saur, while my mother is called *Nan* Saur, which means Saur's mother. In both cultures, parents are not known by their own first names, instead they use a name based on the name of their first son or daughter.

The Orang Rimba are unwilling to take me to the Kemang River. They give various reasons. The path leading to the river passes by the site where a child passed away three years ago, and they say that if they were to go, they would cry out of sadness. My goodness . . . I am so annoyed at them for giving me these bogus reasons. Just give me a map and a compass and I will find it on my own! My only hope is that the two young men who want to go to school will suddenly appear.

March 16, 2000
More illness

On the fifth day of our stay in Bernai, Ngukir (*Bepak* Nangguk) unexpectedly offers to take us to the Kemang River. It takes three hours walking deep into the jungle from our camp at *Bepak* Sejangkang's field. The group at the Kemang River, made up of nine families with a total of 54 people, is led by *Bepak* Melurai who is also a *Depati*.

When we arrive, we find that *Bepak* Melurai's group is just as unwell as the *rombong* of *Temenggung* Bedinding Besi. My previous assumption is correct then, the Orang Rimba are afraid to come here because they fear the disease. We also have a problem finding someone to guide us out of the area. We stay for two days. Throughout this time not a single person joins us or shows any pleasure at our presence.

The two young men who had previously displayed an eagerness to learn do not even show their faces. I am quite irritated. Why are these people afraid? They are so unlike the people I have met in Javanese villages who welcome strangers, generously providing them with food and conversation. Here, forget being hospitable. When Orang Rimba walk by, their faces are grim and creased like folded paper. From a distance, I can hear them mumble comments about how I brought disease, bad omens and so on.

After two days we decide to leave. Initially I persevere; I tell Diki I have no problem staying on my own. Diki stands firm, having seen for himself how are ignoring us. "What if you are mauled by a bear or devoured by a tiger?" he asks. I counter, "Really! I'll be fine. If this is the *rombong* of the two young men, maybe they will show up soon."

Diki insists we wait until this group recovers their health before discussing a school. When they are well, we can return to speak with the chief. I remain impatient.

We travel to a nearby group at Sako Keranji River, headed by *Bepak* Megang. Oh my . . . they are even meaner to us here. I am totally rejected; they explain that this is because I am a woman. They say quite judgmentally, while turning their faces away with indifference, "*Pada kami Orang Rimba, tidak ada orang betina bertugay, cuma orang jenton bae.*" (For us Orang Rimba, there is no such thing as a woman working on her own, only men can do that.)

I realize then that during my previous visits it was all a pretense. All the reasons for denying me assistance were complete lies. They rejected my offer to visit them not because I am a woman but because they really do not want an education—it is perceived as practically useless. I feel discouraged. Even if there are groups who want an education, they must be located at the unreachable ends of the earth. Regardless, one day I will reach them.

In the end, I walk back towards our campground. When I get there, I find that Diki and *Pak* Zul have already moved to a different location and I am left on my own. The distance between my hut and *Indok* Sejangkang's is about 200 meters, but across a big river. In the evening, the whole family visits me for a coffee and a chat. We are still unfamiliar with each other and there is a bit of awkwarness. That night I sleep alone in the hut.

March 18, 2000
The attitude of Orang Rimba children toward their parents

It is acceptable for Orang Rimba children to argue and even berate their parents. I am quite taken aback this morning to see how a child, named Betingkar, ignores his mother when she asks him to fish. He just nonchalantly walks away crinkling his nose—I remember this particular gesture because it is typical of Orang Rimba when they are engaged in uninteresting conversations—while mumbling something incoherent. The mother repeats the demand and the child snaps back harshly, *"Akeh sogoonn!! Kawan bae delok dedewek!!"* (I'm lazy!! You go and find it yourself!!) He snaps at her with a glare, slamming a bundle of branches to the ground.

"Oh my god!" I think, "How rude!" My impulse is to rap him on the head. If this were to happen outside the jungle, young Betingkar might receive a curse that he turn into stone like *Malin Kundang*. In Indonesian folklore, *Malin Kundang* is the ungrateful child who is cursed by his mother whom he had forgotten. Oddly enough, instead of the mother getting angry, she calls her son a lazy sloth with a smile. *"Budak bujang penyogon, todo hopi bulih bini!"* (Lazy-ass child! You'll never find a wife!)

Hearing her words, young Betingkar also smiles. Both of them then look at me with cheerful faces as if to say, "Look at us! Aren't we a happy family?" Hmm, their behavior is adorable yet vexing.

While staying with this family, I learn how children relate to parents in their daily life. I observe that every child has the right to defy their parent's orders or wishes, and has the right to be angry. I also see how Rimba children are taught to gather their own food. Even so, *Bepak* and *Indok* are not upset if the child refuses to search for food and prefers to laze around the *sudung*. I see the unique relationship between Orang Rimba parents and their children, however, there is one key aspect I still do not understand. How do parents educate their children about the Orang Rimba way of life?

When I ask *Indok* Sejangkang about the significance of having a son or daughter, she responds, *"Akeh lebih suka kalu anak akeh betina, kerna orang nang todo tiba podo awok, besemendo, porut awok pula konyong."* (I prefer a daughter, because when a man comes to take her hand, our stomachs will be full.) This is due to their concept of marriage—the husband stays and lives with the wife's family.

I bathe in the river and the two youngest boys of *Indok* Sejangkang gawk and jeer at me from the river's edge. They refuse to budge and ignore my protests. I am completely infuriated. Never in my life has anyone ogled at me while I bathe, not even when I was a child. Ugh, they are really little devils. I try to express my annoyance to *Indok* Sejangkang with good humor. "Au *Indok, akeh marah. Betingkar dengan Besunting haruy bayar dendo, lah mengintip betina mandi!*" ("Yes *Bu*, I am upset. Betingkar and Besunting should be punished for peeping at a woman bathing!")

Both children look tense, and I purposely ignore them. Perhaps they are just curious children, intrigued to discover how people from the outside world bathe or what we look like naked. Still, I dislike being watched as though I am on display or a circus animal. Besides, I wasn't naked. I abide by the jungle custom that it is forbidden to be naked when bathing, a covering cloth is always used. The following day, *Indok* tells me that both her sons are afraid to meet me. They avoid me for two days straight. Finally, I approach them and say that they do not have to act this way. Despite that, there still remains some distance between us.

Indok accompanies me through the day. Sometimes we just chat in front of her hut. She seems calmer than the other mothers in the tribe and smiles a lot. Although I cannot say that she is the quiet type, one thing is for sure, she does not nag as loudly as the other Rimba women. While her husband hunts or taps rubber trees, we sit with the children who play around freely. Once in a while, they timidly join in our conversations. I remain cool but friendly. I always keep in mind my mother's strategy for getting the attention of young children: ignore them!

In time, *Indok* Sejangkang and her family ask me to live with them for the last two days of my visit. I am given a place about a meter wide to sleep near the hearth of their *sudung*. Ah, I feel elated! This is the first time I am allowed to live in their hut. *Indok* says that she is worried about me being alone. She is even more worried about the illegal loggers who sometimes pass through here. I agree, feeling quite good about myself. Ah, it's good to know that someone worries about me . . . .

My relationship with the children is progressing nicely. We play with a *mercon*. This is a matchstick placed below a nail that you thump hard using a piece of wood to make an explosion. It's similar to a firecracker.

I also cook with the family using their kitchen utensils and share meals with them. When they are about to boil some cassava, I volunteer to fry it instead. I was planning to cook at my hut using my own oil but they discreetly fry one portion of cassava especially for me and then share a plate of boiled cassava among the five of them. Apparently they don't like fried cassava. Good for them, I think, less fat.

In the evening after supper, we sit together and they ask me questions "What is the sea like?" or "What kind of fish swim in the sea?" We chat until one o'clock in the morning. They interrupt often while I explain things. As I am falling asleep, I can still hear the children asking *Indok* what whales, sharks and dolphins look like. They ask whether the fish are nasty or not, or delicious to eat and so on. If Indok cannot answer, she hollers, "Bonteeet!!! What are those man-eating fish you were talking about? Sharks or whales?" I smile in quiet amusement, such a nice family.

The following day I bid farewell. *Indok* Sejangkang entrusts me with her broken watch to be repaired, a watch that I am almost certain she can't read. I am a little concerned with this request because I am not sure when I will come back to this *rombong* or the area near the Kemang river.

I find this community quite complex to understand.

March 20, 2000
Orang Rimba receive medical treatment

Finally, my travels bring me to *Temenggung* Bedinding Besi's *rombong*. I feel welcome as soon as I arrive here, although the chief is still grieving over the death of his grandchild. It is quite possible that *Datuk Wakil* Tuha, at Belambun Pupus River (a tributary of the Bernai River), told them about me; Bontet Nangoy, the one who eats Orang Rimba food.

Over the past two weeks there were two deaths in this *rombong*. The first was the grandson of the *temenggung*, a young man of 20. The second was an *Indok* who had two children. During their time of mourning, the community is made even more miserable by the illnesses plaguing them. Everyone is infected except *pesaken Bepak* Sejangkang.

I decide to base myself in the village, at the home of *Pak* Pariyan, because it is only a half-hour walk from the palm oil plantation where the *melangun* is taking place. I also prefer the village because camping in the palm oil plantation is unpleasant and not very secure. During my last visit, the oil workers harassed and teased me. The village health official, *Ibu* Silitonga, confirms my choice of residence. She tells me that pharyngitis (that what she assumed the *rombong* had) is quite dangerous and highly contagious. So the decision is made; I might as well be safe in the village, even though I sometimes feel safer in the depths of the jungle.

The moment I arrive at the *Temenggung*'s house, thirteen-year-old Melabatu, whom I had met on my last trip along the Kemang River, approaches me and says, *"Nio rajo betina, Bontet! Au, nang makon nangoy yoya!"* (Here is the royal Bontet! Ya, the one who ate the boar!) *Temenggung* looks at me and asks whether this is true.

O yeah! I forgot to mention about the first time we introduced ourselves. I ask their names one by one. Several times I make the mistake of asking the name of a young girl. They all just yelled and reprimanded me harshly. It is taboo for the Orang Rimba to say a baby's name if the baby is less than three years old or to mention a young girl's name or to state the name of the dead.

I have difficulty recalling their names. Some I find quite strange. I jot them down in my notebook along with their characteristics. The child with the scar on his head is Bepiyan, the bald one is Ngelambu, the one with long, shaggy hair is Linca, the one with the incessant runny nose, is Pelesir. I slowly learn almost all the names, at least those that are not taboo to say aloud.

They are surprised at how good my memory is. When I test myself by pointing to individuals saying, *"Yoya* Lemago, *yoya* Ejam, *yoya* Sekodi"* (This is Lemago, this is Ejam, and this is Sekodi) they ask me how I can remember more than thirty names in less than half an hour. "I use my pen to make notes," I say. Without realizing it, with this simple skill I leave them in awe.

Soon, a cheeky idea comes into my head. Remembering names might be an incentive for them to learn reading and writing. Earlier at Tengkuyungon, they were quite amazed when I recited their prayer chant while climbing up the honey tree for harvesting. Well, now I can continue to amaze them by reading them my mother's letter, a storybook about the history of the Jambi Kingdom, funny comics about animals and the names of the members of the Orang Rimba groups nearby from surveys conducted by WARSI. For sure, they will not be able to remember all these names within five minutes. They will really have to think hard to recall them at all. It only takes me one minute to read all the names. What is going through their minds? I see a glimmer of an opportunity to introduce the value of reading and writing.

It is quite distressing to see the state of their health. I count seven people who were unable to move and two who have been reduced to just skin and bones because they refuse to eat. My eyes fill with tears seeing their condition and the Orang Rimba find this surprising. I decide to contact Melabatu to find a doctor. He takes an *ojek* (a motorcycle taxi) to Transmigration Unit B to ask for help in treating two children. He succeeds in persuading *Ibu Mantri* Silitonga, the doctor, to come to treat them this very afternoon after her scheduled visit to another patient at Transmigration Unit A. I propose enthusiastically that everyone who is ill will be treated. However, I notice they are hesitant due to the cost of treatment and their lack of funds.

We agree to meet at Transmigration Unit A. I arrive early to locate the house of the patient in need of medical attention. There, I try to persuade *Ibu Mantri* to discount the cost of treatment. I have heard rumors from the villagers that medical treatment outside the government clinics is expensive, even more so for the Orang Rimba. It seems that the Orang Rimba pay a high price because health officials think that they have money.

I try to think of a way to have all the Orang Rimba in this *rombong* treated even though I know that they don't have the means to pay for treatment. I notice that the cost of treatment for the village inhabitants is Rp. 20,000 (around US$2) while for the Orang Rimba it is Rp. 30,000 (around US$3).

It turns out that *Ibu Mantri* is familiar with WARSI and knows Dr. Yanto who used to work here. I pretend that I also know this doctor. Since *Ibu Mantri* and I happen to be from the same *Batak* clan, we speak in our *Batak* dialect so that neither the village people nor the Orang Rimba understand us. I have not spoken Batak since my grandmother's death, so my language skills are quite rusty. We call each other *"Eda"* a title for *Batak* women meaning "sister".

Ibu Mantri grumbles about the usual practice of the Orang Rimba pretending not to have any money. She claims that the medication is not free and was purchased with private funds for around Rp. 3,500. I don't take too much notice of the costs. I am totally preoccupied with trying to figure out how to have the Orang Rimba treated, even by injection if that is necessary. I plead with *Ibu Mantri*. *"Eda* whatever the amount, I will pay. As long as there are receipts. I will process a request through the Health Department at Bangko. If they do not reimburse me, I will ask WARSI. And if they still refuse, I will pay with my own money." To be honest, I am now becoming quite anxious. What if it turns out to be very expensive? My honorarium is only Rp. 500,000 per month (around US$50).

The doctor becomes a little concerned, hearing that I am planning to take the receipts to the Health Department. Perhaps she is worried that her practice of charging higher fees to the Orang Rimba will be discovered. If that is the case, she has asked for it! Finally the treatment cost is reduced from Rp. 30,000 to Rp.10,000 per person, including injections, for five people and Rp. 5,000, without injections, for two more.

Temenggung's wife passes me her money ahead of time, so that I can pay the doctor. I refuse and *Ibu Mantri* notices. I try to have the payment counted openly. The village people who watch the procedure seem somewhat envious of the lower charge. *Ibu Mantri* is looking highly stressed. "Just pay my out-of-pocket costs, little sister," she says.

The Orang Rimba believe that once injected they will recover immediately. I smile in amusement. They look at me warmly, but of course there is no verbal expression of thanks. The words for "thank you" do not exist in the Orang Rimba vocabulary. Yet, from that day on, I feel they have finally started to trust me.

I visit them the next day. When I check their dosage of medication, I find they had muddled up all the instructions. Fortunately, I had taken notes for each individual because I had suspected this would happen.

They take one type of medicine with the dosage for another medication. They share their medicine with each other. The adults share their medicine with children, giving them adult dosages. If some of them feel their medicine is not effective, they exchange it for a different type of medicine from someone who is already feeling better. There is even one child who seems delirious from too much medication. It turns out he had taken the adult dosage of medicine for a different ailment altogether.

If only they could read words, letters and numbers. While I enjoy being here it is impossible for me to check on their medication daily or monthly. And what about when they go to sell their rainforest products? Will I have to accompany them to market as well? Ah, forget it. As the saying goes, God will guide the brave.

I suggest to *temenggung,* on the advice of *Ibu Mantri,* that if they wish I could make a request to the Public Heath Clinic of Transmigration Unit B to have a mobile clinic visit them for just Rp. 2,000 per person. *Temenggung* seems enthusiastic. Then he adds that they will have to wait for the sale of the rubber sap this week. He says that money is short because he has 30 lengths of *koin* (textiles), which are still unsold. He also complains that it had been a while since they had any meat in their diet.

March 24, 2000
As easy as riding a bicycle

Today Berenoy insists that I ride the bicycle belonging to sixteen-year-old Ejam. He says, *"Mikay melawon, betina tapi tokang besepeda."* (You are amazing, being a girl yet able to ride a bicycle.) He asks me to teach him how to ride. Only three young people in this *rombong* know how to ride a bike. I teach four children until the tires burst and I am out of breath from chasing them.

I ask one of the mothers about the type of rattan needed to make an *ambung*. I also ask her permission to write down the step-by-step process. As I am doing this, the children gather around me. While I am talking, one of the children takes my pen and pretends to write, while the others start a ruckus trying to snatch it. They ask how to write their names. They tell me that Amilda, the WARSI anthropologist, has taught them several letters. For example, *kerakai* (branch) represents the letter k, *perut gendut* (fat-belly), the letter b and *kail* (hook), the letter j. They say they would like to try to copy more letters.

Every time the Orang Rimba children take my pen they run far away and try to write or draw. Eventually, they timidly show me what they have done. They laugh at their friend's work if I correct it. I am also aware of the adults who are intently watching my every word and move while the youngsters giggle. I hold my breath. Dear Lord, I hope that I don't make a stupid mistake this time.

Bepak Bepiun, who is standing watching us says, *"Belajarlah mikai galo menuliy?"* (Why don't all of you learn how to write?) He asks me, *"Apo budak-budak yoya todo depot tokang menuliy?"* (Will all the children be able to write like this?)

I answer, *"Samolah dengan pelajoron besepeda, kalu blajor, todo tokang jugo."* (Just like learning to ride a bicycle, if one tries, eventually it will happen.)

He asks again, *"Au . . . apo kalo satu bulan belajar lah tokang menuliy?"* ("Ya . . . would one month be enough to teach them to write?")

I answer as best I can, *"Bisa jugolah."* ("It is possible.")

Oh my goodness, one month? He must be kidding. I had to bash my brother's head for a year for him to learn to read. I remember asking Ejam how long it took him to master riding a bicycle. He said one month. Using my analogy *Bepak* Bepiun must have assumed literally that learning reading and writing would take just as long.

March 25, 2000
Why leave so soon?

I notice the Orang Rimba are crowded around *temenggung's sudung*. I see that *temenggung's* wife cannot get up because her liver is swollen. She is being treated by a shaman called Munte, who happened to pass by on his way to his fields. Quietly, I grimace. Ah, why didn't she go for treatment to *Ibu Mantri* a few days ago? I see Bedinding Besi shake his head several times saying, *"Kami kena bala, Tuhan marah pada kami."* (A catastrophe has befallen us, God is angry with us.).

Temenggung's wife asks what is wrong with her and what is the cure. I explain the ailment to her, all the while massaging her feet and legs to relax her. I also tell her that I am leaving today to go to Bangko. "Why do you want to leave so soon?" she asks. I quickly explain that plans were already put into place before I arrived. I assure her that she will recover soon.

While I have only been with this group for five days, I have been in the jungle for two weeks traveling and visiting other groups. My allotted time is up and I am expected back as planned. The office transport will soon collect me at *Pak* Pariyan's family home. She kisses my hand when I say goodbye, which surprises me. Perhaps she feels close or wishes to show a gesture of respect. *Temenggung* asks me if I will pray for his wife. I respond jokingly, *"Apo dewo akeh dengan dewo Orang Rimba samo apo hopi?"* (Is my God the same as your Orang Rimba God?) *"Samo baelah, Ibu,"* (It is all the same, *Ibu,*) he replies.

I inform my coordinator that medical personnel are urgently needed for the Orang Rimba. There has been an increase in the range of diseases they are subjected to as the quality of their river water worsens and the rainforest progressively shrinks, loses its animals or suffers other changes that impact them. Also, most Orang Rimba do not understand how to obtain the services of the government clinics. Their present level of customary knowledge is not adequate to cope with all this.

I am determined to stay close to this group. The future prospects with them are promising because of their number and age range. More importantly, I feel reasonably welcome and I like them. Unfortunately, they are to go on a *melangun* within the next three months. Although it will take place around the accessible Tanagaro Transmigration Unit A, I doubt whether they will be willing to take up reading and writing while grieving.

I will wait and see. I am apprehensive but also excited.

Chapter 5

Ibu, Give Us a School

April 13, 2000
Back to the jungle

Today, I must return to the rainforest. The day I depart is always hectic. Many people from the transmigration villages send requests to buy things to bring back for them. They ask for pots, sarongs, dozens of plates for parties, plastic cabinets, even bicycles. As a result, the back of the office jeep is loaded to the roof.

All along the pot-holed roads, people shout out, "Are you selling on credit, *Mbak*?" Normally I react casually, shaking my head. This only prompts another question, "Oh, you only take cash? Over here then, I would like to see your goods!" Geez . . . don't they understand?

Despite teasing from my WARSI colleagues, I am quite happy to ease the burden of these transmigrants living over seventy kilometers from Bangko. Quite often, I deliver the goods to those who requested them and ask for a payment below my actual purchase price. The bigger the discount, the happier they are, and the prouder I am at having done a good deed. It puzzles me why I have this impulse. My mother used to scold me every time I ran a small business; I always ended up with a loss having given away too many things.

The *Temenggung* Bedinding Besi *rombong* is still taking part in a *melangun*. The group has moved from the palm oil plantation near the Bernai River to the rubber plantation near the transmigrant housing along Flamboyan Road in Tanagaro. The *melangun* has been going for about a month at the palm oil plantation. There are already nine *bubungon* roofs made of black plastic sheeting. Each is separated from the next by five to fifteen meters. This small, occupied area, spread out over about twenty square kilometers, is only one kilometer from the Trans-Flamboyan Road. This main road has to be crossed regularly to collect water located up a path on the other side.

Despite the persistent cough among most of the *rombong* community, health conditions have improved and they are not suffering from flu-like symptoms anymore. They often eat meat, such as pork or squirrel, and they always remember to put some aside for me. This time, I stay in *Ibu* Pariyan's house, about one-and-a-half kilometers away from the group. I normally walk or cycle to their camp, taking the shortcut through the hilly rubber plantation.

I am still using anthropological methods to get to know the Orang Rimba. This makes me feel distant from them. Do I need the trappings of anthropology to succeed here? The structured approach to understanding people only confuses me.

I remember doing research for my undergraduate paper in West Timor. I left most of my research equipment untouched in my bag because I ended up just playing around with the "subjects" of my research. Having made many acquaintances there, I delved into their daily activities for three months, but without documenting any important information. At the end of my fieldwork, when I returned to Bandung and met my lecturer, he was astounded at how little I had documented.

"What the hell did you do there?" He immediately ordered me to return to the field. Instead of being sad, I was quite pleased with his decision. I taught some classes, saved money, and returned to the field the following year. This time, I worked really hard to collect a lot of data by interview, questionnaire, participant observer approach, but, in the end, I didn't have a clue what I was going to do with it. He he he . . . I had no idea how to analyze all the data using anthropological methods. Finally, one of my professors helped me with my analysis.

Remembering my lecturer's disappointment, I am determined to absorb whatever I can learn from the experiences of the last few months. Some of the events that took place, for example, helping the Orang Rimba to obtain cheap medication, make me think deeply about the people and their daily existence. But, I do not want my interactions to be bound by complicated agendas.

I came here to do something meaningful, so there is not an urgent need for me to read or write, or to stick to strict anthropological approaches like structuralism, determinism or whatever . . . nonsense! I just want to make friends and let things flow without worrying about gauging my success using assessment standards. I just want things to happen naturally.

I live in a jungle with its inhabitants, and if they befriend me I'll see what I can do to help them.

April 17, 2000
Just playing around

Unexpectedly, my desire to get closer to the Orang Rimba gains momentum on its own. Seven children begin pressuring me to immediately start teaching them numbers and the alphabet. I am quite concerned about the views of the parents who are constantly watching me. While they don't yell at me, as I thought they might, they are still suspicious. I have to teach the children surreptitiously, as if teaching is not my main mission here. In fact, it is no longer my primary objective!

I give the children scrap paper to scribble on and use an alphabet book with letters and numbers from zero to nine in a large font. I try to divert their attention so that they will not always ask me about the alphabet. An elderly woman comes to me and says, "*Sokola hopi ado dalam adat kami, kalu kami keno bala, yoya ketinye kamu nang bikin kedulat!*" (School is not in our tradition, if calamity befalls us; you are the one who has caused our damnation!) I just grin and nod in agreement.

Throughout the first week, I just play with the children. I visit them, we eat together, and I teach them to sing the 'names of the days' song and the alphabet song. They surprise me when they sing pop tunes and *dangdut* dance songs. I also teach them how to sew, to ride a bike and to do a martial arts sequence called *pencak silat*. In exchange, they teach me how to make a mat of *seluang* leaves and how to prepare *guntor*, a local fruit. Sometimes we fish for catfish in the river, deep in the rainforest.

These are my daily activities and I enjoy them very much. Over time, I realize just how much I enjoy being around children.

April 19, 2000
One week in the field

This afternoon when I return home on *Ibu* Pariyan's bike, several Rimba children stand waiting for me at the house where I am staying. They arrived earlier because they took a shortcut. They want to continue their bike-riding lessons. The one bicycle they had, which belonged to Ejam, was sold, so the bike I am riding is their only option. They take turns learning to ride the bike. Not only do they use *Ibu* Pariyan's bicycle, they also borrow some from her neighbors.

April 22, 2000
"Ibu, give us a school"

Yesterday, while I was at the palm oil plantation with the Orang Rimba, a truck passed by and several children hitched a ride to the transmigration village instead of coming for a bike-riding lesson with me. One of the children, Besudu, had apparently broken the handlebars of the only bike, so the children were headed to the village to ride their friends' bikes.

Today, *Indok* Besudu comes on her own initiative with Besudu and Ngelambu, bringing a piece of cloth to pay for the repair. Besudu looks terrified; he has been crying all morning from being yelled at by his mother. He says that he has been punished and he had to go without food. He has not eaten anything since the previous day. He confides that his family does not have any money to pay for the bike repair.

The cost of the repair is double—two pieces of cloth because the value of each cloth is Rp. 15,000 and the price to repair the handlebars is Rp. 17,500. The bicycle owner seems displeased with the compensation, so I feel compelled to pay him in cash. I take back the cloth, without telling the Orang Rimba. After this incident, the children are not allowed to cycle anymore. When I propose restarting this activity, the adults only allow those who can already ride to participate.

Nevertheless, I continue teaching the children, especially the beginners. We still have only six children who are competent riders.

Success in learning to ride provides an example for the children to apply while they are learning new concepts. I use this example to motivate them to study counting and the alphabet. *"Segelonya sejak dari mulaknya hopi tokang, tapi kalu pelajoron turuy, jadi tokang!"* (Everything starts with inexperience, and through the process of learning, over time one becomes an expert!)

I observe that they are now keen to read and write. When they ask me questions about anything I turn my answer into a learning opportunity. For example, my digital watch becomes a stimulus to learn to recognize numbers. Most of the children are already familiar with analog watches. At first, they only read time with the hour hand. Then, by always counting from the top, where the number is closest to the brand name, they begin to tell the time.

When they first see my digital watch, they ask about the shapes of the numbers. I draw the numbers in a book and they borrow my pen to mimic the shapes. They push and shove each other, fighting to write the numbers and read them out loud. I tell them about the different ways the world outside the jungle uses numbers for various purposes, including writing the amount of money in a transaction.

"What about letters, *Ibu*?" one asks, "How are they used?"

The children seem really enthusiastic. I begin to tell them how to use the alphabet, how letters make up words and then sentences to create descriptions. But then, as usual, I quickly divert their attention to other things. I am afraid their enthusiasm for numbers and the alphabet will boomerang against me, and I want to prevent that.

We continue with our martial arts lesson instead, and they ask me about the sports of the outside world. They try to imitate my movements, but are as stiff as robots. The funny thing is that this is only the warm-up routine. When we start learning the core movements, they all complain, "I cannot do it, Ibu! My entire body is sore!"

We take a break. Since there is nothing else to do, I take out my diary and pen and start writing. I notice that when I am writing, they are whispering among themselves. Suddenly, one of the children, Batu, approaches me and says, *"Ibu beri kami Sokola!"* (*Ibu*, give us a school!) These words sound so beautiful.

"Uh . . . What?!" I am shocked at this straightforward request. It is happening too fast. I think the parents might rebuke me again; they really like to express discontent when it came to reading and writing. I am not ready to lose this progress.

"Can't you go to the school in the next village?" I ask.

"We don't want to. The teachers in the village school punish us and they are too serious. We would like you to be our teacher if you can come to the jungle," one student explains.

It is my turn now to feign disinterest, *"Ya,* we'll see. I don't want to get into trouble with the elders."

In reality, I am terrified. I have enjoyed their friendship and the process of getting to know each another. Our reciprocal gestures of learning have been invaluable and unique. I do not want to ruin this relationship by rushing into an introduction to literacy.

April 23, 2000
Shy Rimba kids

At around six a.m. this morning, three children, Besudu (15), Batu (13), and Linca (14) surprise me by coming to *Ibu* Pariyan's house to see me. The first child, Batu, has one hand inside his clothes hiding something, which turns out to be a pencil. He hid it because he is embarrassed to be seen with it by my host family. The book that I gave him the day before is folded several times and tucked inside the pocket of his shorts. He whispers to me that he wants to learn writing. They prefer writing here, instead of at their camp, for fear of being discovered by their parents.

I signal that I would rather not start right away because members of *Ibu* Pariyan's family are still around. So we just spend the time chatting. They seem uncomfortable so I try to lighten the atmosphere by telling stories of the outside world. We start our studies in earnest after most of the members of *Ibu* Pariyan's family finally leave the house.

Whenever any member of the family passes by or glances at their books, they immediately stop, cover their writing, and stare at me, protesting. *"E, akeh hopi ndok ibu, todo!"* (Aah! Please don't look at it, *Ibu*, I'll show you later!) They feign disinterest in the lessons, but resume work once the person has left. I try to make *Ibu* Pariyan's family understand so they will ignore the children and just continue doing their own thing. Meanwhile the kids explain, *"Akeh kemaloun, sebab akeh hopi tokang menuliy, ibu."* (I'm embarrassed, *Ibu*, because I'm really bad at writing.)

Actually, I don't have any formal experience teaching basic reading, writing or math. The only experience I have was teaching my brother, who I incessantly pinched, until he grimaced and could not focus. Things might get ugly if I start to pinch these children!

I feel I should do an internship at the primary school in the nearby village. Then, I remember meeting a child who was already in their fourth year at the school but still could not read or write. How can that be? What were they doing for four years?

April 24, 2000
School, day two

On the second day of "school", the number of students increases to seven. I illustrate addition using drawings and stories and keep the totals to less than twenty. I notice that the children understand addition faster when I illustrate the concept with stories or by counting money. I also mention briefly the concept and logic of larger numbers. I introduce them to the idea of tens, hundreds, thousands, ten thousands, hundred thousands and millions. I make a provisional chalkboard out of a slab of wood and use charcoal as chalk. I give them little quizzes with similar problems and let them compete and laugh at each other.

April 25, 2000
"How much longer before I can read?"

On the third day, only three students show up, Batu, Linca and Lemago. Maybe the other four children dropped out because they were being laughed at so often. Unbelievable! I feel badly for those four children. They were teased because their "slowness" bothered the other students. The rest said they were bored with learning to count and were ready to learn reading. Batu is the best at counting. His only problem is confidence. While he always responds timidly, his answers are almost always correct. In general, they all have good memories and are energetic.

As for school supplies, I try using the materials available in the jungle around us, but I soon realize that paper is more effective. Paper can be saved as a record and it is easier to review paper than scribbles on the trees, the ground or on mud walls, which are too easily erased. Notes on paper or in books can also be re-used to teach other children. Nevertheless, we still use materials found in nature for practice.

The most annoying thing for me is the constant, repetitive questioning when we are in the middle of working or when I compliment them on a correct answer, *"Jadi ini ibu, berapo lamo lagi akeh tokang membaca?"* (Now then, *Ibu*, how much longer before I can read?)

April 27, 2000
Looking for a structured approach

I begin to experience the same difficulties encountered by Yusak. The Orang Rimba have an amazing capacity for memorization—they learn the alphabet in a span of just a few hours. However, they have difficulty connecting the letters for spelling. I completely run out of ideas on how to explain this concept to them. I simply teach them how to spell words they want to read, but I do not have a structured approach. On my last day in the jungle, I try a new method of pronouncing letters, repeating them at increasing speeds. This seems to be more effective, although it may be a coincidence.

For example, the word PENA (pen) is formed by the letters P-E-N-A. The children begin to comprehend this when I repeat the four letters at faster and faster speeds. Then we try the same method with BATU (stone) and TOPI (hat). Eventually, they understand these sequences! But when they spell my name, BUTET, or KERTAS (paper), they are at a loss again.

There must be a more methodical and structured way to teach spelling and reading. Intuitively, I am convinced that I am not the first to experience this kind of barrier. There must be some book or guide on the subject that has the answer. I think that I will probably find a "how to" teacher's guidebook at the primary school at Bangko.

Chapter 6

My Students Are My Teachers

May 9, 2000
Fear

After twelve days away, I return from Bangko and arrive at the Tanagaro Transmigration Unit A. Soon after my arrival, I start to receive threats and stories sprinkled with warnings. The village people had come to talk to *Ibu* Pariyan and to my students. They were not complimentary and told many lies about me. There were also threats from the illegal loggers. They apparently said, "What is Butet doing here? Tell her to behave if she wants to be safe." I assume the latter threats came from loggers who have children working for them as bonded servants. I believe "slaves" is a more apt description.

Hearing these stories and warnings makes me anxious. What happens if they follow through with their threats? I tell myself not to give into my fear. I need to articulate and understand the cause of my fear in order to manage it better. Isn't it true that in whatever you set out to accomplish, if you have a clear objective, you won't easily be distracted? I know that my objective in coming here is to establish a jungle school. I also know that fear is part of any challenge and can serve a useful purpose. In this instance, I cannot and will not allow myself to be defeated by fear alone.

Later the villagers and some of my students tell me the timber merchants are asking questions about me. "How long will she stay? Why is she here?" They make other comments too, essentially saying, "Watch out, don't meddle in our work!"

To me, their warnings sound like a mother telling her child who is climbing a tree, "Watch out! Don't climb trees or you might fall!" A child normally replies, "But what if I don't fall?" This is how children reason. They can only see the rewarding aspect of things. Now, what is the problem with that? If you think only of the worst-case scenarios, when will you be free to experience those exciting and pleasurable things that require some risk taking? When is the right time to climb a tree? What happens if you do fall? Well, you hit the ground . . . he he he. So Butet, look at this positively and don't let fear stop your progress.

I have gone through the highs and lows of getting to know the people in this unique Orang Rimba group at *Temenggung* Bedinding Besi. Our relationship is akin to the flavor of *Nano-Nano* candy—sweet, salty and tangy. The people of *Temenggung* Bedinding Besi have moved back again to the palm oil plantation twenty minutes to the south of the Tanagaro Transmigration Unit. This was earlier than expected because one of the villagers died and was buried somewhere near their last *melangun*. Tradition calls for the Orang Rimba to stay far away from the burial sites of the dead. Although the dead man was not an Orang Rimba, the *rombong* were uneasy and felt compelled to move again to shield themselves from any potential misfortune.

May 10, 2000
A reading performance

I am anxious to see if my re-appearance will be greeted warmly or whether I will have to suffer like before. In my worst-case scenario, I have to start back at zero again. The children may have forgotten what they learned last month. I prepare myself mentally, including the possibility that I will go home if circumstances are too difficult. I don't think I can start all over again. While I am not optimistic about the possibility of continuing with my teaching, my previous stay at *rombong Temenggung* Bedinding Besi was friendly and I want to keep the line of friendship alive.

My first task on arrival is to look up my notes to remind myself of the boys' names. Once again they are amazed that I can still remember each and every one.

The wife of the *Temenggung* (*Indok* Berenoy) brings out some papers held by the family, which they call the *piagam* (charter). She asks me to read them. It takes me half an hour to get through them all. I find one item particularly interesting—*Jenang* Rio Sayuti's writing entitled *Asal Usul Makekal*, which might be translated as *The Origin of Immortality*. This story chronologically recounts the historical relationship between the Orang Rimba and the *Orang Terang*. There is a history of *Temenggung Jenang* Rio and a record of the customary law of the Orang Rimba, *undang nan delapan* (the eight laws), which is recognized by most village heads. There is also a record of all the agreements and sworn promises that have been made between *Jenang* Rio and the Orang Rimba. *Indok*

89

Berenoy asks me many times to repeat parts of the charter she thinks are important, while the children listen attentively and with reverence.

In the afternoon, when it is time to return to my room, five children come with me and ask me to teach them to read the alphabet right away because they only mastered part of the alphabet the previous month.

May 11, 2000
How to teach reading?

From that day on, after going into the rainforest in the mornings to check on the animal traps they set, the children come to the house at the Tanagaro Transmigration Unit and study until evening; sometimes even late into the night.

I read an Indonesian grammar book for primary school, which I had purchased in a bookshop at Bangko. Unfortunately, it does not help very much. Maybe the book is out of date as it was published about ten years earlier. I am not sure why it doesn't work, but the information seems to be all over the place with gaps between key points. It is like a recipe book listing all the ingredients—chili peppers, onions, candlenut, and shrimp paste—but not providing any explanation about how the ingredients are used. With this information, you still need to research the characteristics and flavor of the ingredients before you can produce a meal!

I prefer to teach my students how the letters are phonologically formed through a process of logical reasoning rather than mimicking. I develop a more structured teaching strategy with a rules-based approach to letters and their corresponding sound. I explain why the letter *M* can't be voiced when the nose is closed. I demonstrate why a series of consonant letters cannot be read together and how they need to be connected by a vowel.

I was never taught language in this logical way when I was little. I just drew on what I heard. During my university linguistics courses, I learned that the rules of phonetics could clarify the logical processes associated with pronunciation. I begin to think that my lessons can be simplified and made more effective. I just need to figure out how to explain this to the children. They are such quick learners, but obviously I will need to use words and concepts that are appropriate for children. It would be absurd to use terms such as "articulation" or "nasal" or technical words to explain the alphabet or aspects of grammar.

May 13, 2000
Two more students

Ibu Pariyan wakes me up at 6:30 this morning. Two unfamiliar boys, about fourteen years old, have arrived unexpectedly. When I open the door they look at me nervously. They are both neatly dressed. I guess that they are Orang Rimba because of their alert and clear eyes. I immediately give them the sweetest smile I can muster, not wanting to scare them away. Awkward smiles begin to form at the corners of their mouths. "I am Butet. What are your names?" They say their names are Gentar and Miti and they are close friends. Then, they whisper their intentions.

Apparently Gentar's older brother-in-law, Gemeram, saw me when I was buying a notebook at the village shop. He recounted to them my conversation with my students, Batu and the others. He also said that, if they studied with me, they could come and go as they pleased because I didn't hand out punishments. I hold back a grin. So that is the impression they have of me compared to the village school! Wah, I think to myself, I could be arrested by the Ministry of Education.

Surprisingly, they do not want to be in the same study group as Batu and his friends. Gentar said that Batu and the others are *becenenggo* or diseased. They also fear banishment when they return to their group in Bernai. I am quite alarmed when I find out they are from the *rombong Wakil* Tuha. This is the *rombong* that "expelled" me several months ago. Apparently, Gentar and Miti had seen me, but did not have the courage to approach me to teach them in their *rombong*. They thought, for sure, the other members of their group would yell at them.

I notice that these two groups keep a mutual distance from one another. This is a bit strange because they are blood-relatives and friendly toward each other. It is even more confusing to me when I realize that keeping a distance does not only apply in the jungle, but also in this village house. Gentar wants to study behind the house in the hut where the family stores their firewood and bicycle. And so, we sit on top of the pile of wood, while Miti sits on the bicycle writing in his notebook. We make quite a funny sight.

Miti is very observant, curiously watching my every movement and taking notice of every item I have, from my automatic pencil and my fragrant candy-like eraser, to my Walkman cassette player. I feel uncomfortable. I am sure that in his eyes, all these things are rather superfluous. I deliberately make very little use of them and other items in my bag. I do not want to seem strange or very different from them. For some reason, I begin to feel silly having these objects. Every glance from Miti seems to say, "Why do you rely so much on these strange items? Why are there so many? Do you all live like this, you city people?"

Gentar, on the other hand, seems more relaxed. He too observes every object and we discuss my things with great interest. I feel he views me positively for some reason, although we have only just met. He is enthusiastic, cheerful, and willing to do everything I suggest. He readily erases the small writing board and prepares the chalk just like an assistant.

May 14, 2000
Frenzied parents

Today, Miti left at noon with his cousin, who had returned from the market. Gentar went home in the afternoon, while the others stayed on and studied. In the afternoon, *Indok* Nyado, Miti's mother and *Indok* Sedina arrive at my place and immediately go into a raging frenzy, yelling at me for allowing their children to come and study. They insist that I have forced Miti and Gentar to disobey their customs and desecrate nature and that this will bring about disaster. They also say that Miti became ill this afternoon—because of studying.

May 15, 2000
A mother threatens to drink poison

This morning, Gentar arrives alone to start his lessons. Three *bepak* follow in a fury to fetch him back. Apparently, there had been an agreement with the *Depati* that Gentar would be engaged to his daughter, Nyina. They visited *Depati* Laman Senjo twice to enter into the engagement but were refused a meeting. On the third attempt, they were finally accepted. If Gentar refuses now, they will be embarrassed and will have to pay a fine. Gentar is adamant. He refuses to comply, stating, "It is your wish, not mine, you are the stupid ones!" Gentar likes Nyina but thinks that, at fifteen, he is too young to marry.

Around noon, the children from Bedinding Besi *rombong* arrive. We work as usual. When I return to the back of the house, I see that the three *bepak* are still outside reprimanding Gentar. Eventually a decision is made. "If Gentar does not agree to the engagement, if he insists on studying, then Gentar has to leave the jungle."

Upset by all this, Gentar decides to run away. Later this afternoon, he collects his possessions and moves in with Linca and the others at Bedinding Besi. If Linca is kicked out too, they resolve to run away together rather than give up reading and writing. "We follow our *Ibu Guru*," they say. *Waduh*, this is serious! "What if they are really going to follow me?" I think

Toward evening, at around 6.30pm, while Batu, Linca and the others are still studying, *Indok* Nyado, *Indok* Melasau (Gentar' mother), thirteen-year-old Natal and some other young children come over. *Indok* Nyado says that *Indok* Melasau is going to commit suicide because Gentar is not coming home. *Indok* Melasau cries inconsolably, pleading with me to stop teaching Gentar. She asks me to persuade him to come home and to accept the engagement.

She waves around a bottle containing rubber-tree poison, threatening all the while that she will drink it. She says that she is afraid that I will teach all the Rimba children in the rainforest for years, and slowly turn them into village people. I swear a Rimba oath, the same oath *Indok* Nyado said aloud the day before. "If I take away Gentar and Miti, if I move all the Orang Rimba to a village, I will be cursed! If I am in the water, I will be eaten by a crocodile. If I am on land, I will be eaten by a tiger. And, if I am in the jungle, a tree will fall on me!"

After I explain that, I will work with Gentar for a maximum of three months, not for years, she doesn't mind so much if he studies. Now, *Indok* Melasau only fears that Gentar will run away from the jungle. According to *Indok* Melasau, *Wakil* Tuha, who had refused Willi and Hadi's offer of education last February, will not forbid youth from learning reading and writing if the objective is really to prevent them from being cheated. However, if the objective is to transform them into village people or to convert them to Islam, then education violates their customs; they do not want this. The *rombong* inhabitants join in, trying to persuade *Indok* Melasau to be more rational. After all the commotion, the two women and the children finally go home and everyone calms down.

The following day, Gentar comes to study a little later than usual, at around 9:30 am. Everything is settled with the understanding that he is to continue studying, but has to stay in the rainforest. I promise that I will not teach him if he threatens to run away again.

93

May 17, 2000
My students, my teachers

"Ibu, akeh tadi ngoli budak-budak trans unjur sokola. Akeh pikir au samo awok a, akeh pula berangkat sokola." (*Ibu*, I just saw the transmigrant children going to school. I thought, ah, it's the same with us, we also go to school.)

I grimace. Is this place good enough to be called "school"? The very name is a burden. I am afraid I will not be able to fulfill their expectations. Yet, right from the beginning, they always called it *"sokola"*.

I start to teach reading and writing, although still in a haphazard fashion. My methods begin to take shape slowly based on the students' questions. They often bring newspaper clippings or product wrappers with words on them to class and read them haltingly. Reading becomes quite competitive. If there is a dispute about the meaning of the text, they argue with each other, each adamantly demanding that they are right. It can be quite irritating watching them arguing foolishly about something they have read.

Take the case of a child reading *b*, then *u* for the sound bu, and then without reason, without looking at the end of the word, he says, "Ah, this one has to be *buku*," when actually it is *bulan*. Another might say, *"batu"*. They start arguing as if they are experts in the language. Sometimes it is not easy for me to intervene and correct the reader.

It is even trickier for me to organize my teaching time because the students progress at such different speeds. The beginners are still studying their alphabet, while others have progressed to reading and spelling with double letters like BA-BI-BU-BE-BO. Some have begun to learn numbers. Everyone is impatient to master their different areas, each in their own way.

There are times when their questions inspire me. For example, when we came across a word like MALAM or RAMBUT, I found that to divide every word into two-letter chunks did not always work. Every syllable needs one vowel. My university experience and my Linguistic and Anthropology majors helped me to shape a method and teaching structure, that each syllable in Indonesian has its own conditions, that a consonant cannot be read by itself, that one vowel can stand alone as one syllable. However, I have no idea what the necessary building blocks are when one starts from zero. In this case, their questions prompt many ideas. For instance, how many ways of pronunciation exist for every sequence of letters spelling a word in the Indonesian language?

There are some funny cases, too. The Orang Rimba always pronounce words ending with S as a Y. In the reverse case, if the end is a Y then it is pronounced with the ending S. This becomes a problem when I give them reading material. When I ask, "BA + S = what?" they answer, *"BAY"*. I repeat BAS several times, but their answer is still *"BAY"*. I will have to try other methods!

"Now, what is BI + S =?" Eh, the same, they answer again, *"BIY"*. So it continues that way, BUY, BEY, BOY. I change my strategy and ask, "BA + Y =?" I've got you now; you must admit your mistake! Right away they respond, *"BAS"*, straight-faced without any expression of confusion! *Aduhhhh!* I shake my head, running out of ideas. They look at me, worried, and ask, *"Ibu* is something wrong? Why do you look upset?"

It continues like this. Every moment for me is filled with great happiness. Watching them read correctly gives me a strange sense of contentment in my heart; it is an achievement. Yet, at the same time, there is a tiny nagging concern. Am I doing the right thing? They constantly ask questions about this and that. Some overwhelm me and yet highlight all the things they need to know. Slowly, in response to these questions, I can begin to create my lesson material.

Now I begin to classify words into groups. Every time I come across a new syllable, I create a group of words in Rimba and Indonesian based on this new syllable. I use words that are common in day-to-day language or important for specific occasions. I realize that I am improving my Indonesian. I now appreciate that all words are formed by certain combinations of syllables.

This idea begins to consume me. As soon as the children leave, I rush to the well to bathe and then eat dinner. On the way to and from the well and during my bath, all the letters and syllables dance in my head forming lines and groups. I can visualize them clearly. At around seven o' clock in the evening, I start to work out the lesson material, remembering various letter permutations. I write down everything that comes to mind. I track down words starting with the letters A to Y (there is no sound "Z" in Orang Rimba language!)

I am hugely motivated, writing non-stop until the early hours of the morning. At three in the morning, *Ibu* Pariyan wakes up and tells me to go to bed. I finally go to my room feeling guilty for making her plead with me so many times to go to sleep. I enter the bedroom holding the oil lamp and continue working silently. By morning I have finally finished setting up a system of seven classifications, each with hundreds of examples of words. I am not sure if these classifications are representative, but I have given it my best shot this night.

May 18, 2000
Experimenting with my method

I should be sleepy this morning, but on the contrary, I feel light and energetic. I am not hungry, and neither are the children. Only when *Ibu* Pariyan brings us some food do we realize that it is already three in the afternoon. The children's enthusiasm equals my own when I introduce them to the new learning and classification method I created in the middle of the night.

It is a miracle! They easily comprehend what I am teaching them and they are very keen to read each example given. Oh my God, I feel sooooo cool. I cannot even begin to describe this wonderful feeling. I like it, I feel proud and inspired. I will not stop until I can prove that they, these strange but sweet children, CAN read. I cannot wait until we reach the final lesson. Ah, they are so clever, I swear. And I bet that their average comprehension ability is way beyond those in the villages around here. Why is that?

Ibu Pariyan's daughter, Ros who is in second grade, follows me and helps me like an assistant. The children are no longer timid. They ask a lot of questions, trying this word and that. It's funny, two months later; it will be Ros asking Gentar and his friends to teach her how to read words with "ng". Apparently, at her school, words with ng are only taught when students reach third grade.

In the evening, around 8pm, an *Indok* comes by and drops off some food. It is python meat. It has a very interesting taste, simply chopped and boiled with salt and onion. This is the first time I have eaten python. Although it is delicious, the skin is very chewy and I feel like I am eating my own rubber sandals.

May 19, 2000
A fun class

The children come to *Ibu* Pariyan's house daily at six or six thirty in the morning and leave in the evening when the sun sets. They seem to adapt without a hitch to the new reading and writing materials. There is always a slightly competitive atmosphere. Now, none of the students bother to check their traps for animals or to work as guides for loggers or NGO (Non-Governmental Organization) staff. They fear being left behind if they leave while the others are still studying. There are hardly any occasions when they don't concentrate or are not serious. If one gives a wrong answer, the others laugh at him. If one gets ahead of the others, always being first and correct, the others get a little jealous and make fun of him, hit him playfully, or cover his eyes or mouth.

I begin to teach addition. When the children master simple addition using numbers up to ten, they demand to move on to higher numbers. Then they ask what happens if there are more than two items to add together. Wah, this means I have to teach them a system for summing things up.

It is time to teach them simple multiplication. "What is the total if I sell 85 pieces of rattan at Rp. 4,500 per piece, 27 kilos of *damar* wood at Rp. 600 per kilo or seven kilos of honey at the price of Rp. 7,500 per kilo?"

In reality, through the process of working together, we are formulating our own teaching methods and lesson materials through trial and error. Now all I have to do is to give it shape.

May 20, 2000
Scandal

Bedinding Besi, who initially was an ardent supporter of the school, suddenly has a change of attitude toward me. *Ibu* Pariyan and I discover that a timber merchant has scared him. One day, Bedinding Besi asked me to accompany him to a meeting with the Governor to report some illegal timber theft. Later investigations would reveal that he reported only those thefts that failed to pay a bribe or commission to him. The trip never took place because Bedinding Besi was worried that his wheeling and dealing would be discovered.

Today, a timber merchant stops by the house. He acts in a patronizing manner. He does not begin with the customary greetings or even knock at the door; he just enters the house and summons a child who is studying to go and buy some cigarettes and deliver some money. The market is 30 minutes away. I approach him and protest because he is interrupting the child's lesson. He introduces himself off-handedly, and goes on disregarding me. The children are stunned and terrified. The merchant then leaves the house with Bedinding Besi to go to the market and do some shopping.

Then, *Indok* Berenoy asks me whether I will ever send the children to school outside the rainforest. "Is it is true that all Rimba land will be converted to plantations? Will the Orang Rimba be re-settled in the villages?" She then lists all the goods she bought with the money given to her by the timber merchant. Having recounted this, she asks me for money.

I say, "I am not an illegal logger, I don't steal from your rainforest. Why do I have to give you money?"

May 22, 2000
Gastric flu outbreak

Close to the end of my stay in Bangko, some children from Bedinding Besi are hit by *muntaber* or gastroenteritis. I take my motorbike and speed to the nearest mobile government clinic to request some reasonable treatment for these children. The clinic van is under repair and has been in the garage for nearly a month. Despite this, four medical personnel come along by motorbike. When we arrive, the Orang Rimba who have gathered at the TSM house since noon. By five o'clock, twelve Orang Rimba receive medical treatment. I ask the doctors to prepare medical identity cards so that they can go directly to the government clinic in the future for a reasonable fee. I ask the children to distribute the medical cards. They read the cards out loud which makes a very positive impression on the adults.

Dr. Siswadi, the practicing doctor at the Muara Bulian Government Clinic, proposes regular monthly visits. He also suggests an advisory program to work with and enhance the practice of traditional medicine. He recommends that the program be designed to work with the *dukun* or traditional medicine practitioner. Dr. Siswadi is an enlightened man with a taste for adventure, and expresses interest in working for WARSI. Health issues are actually under the administration of WARSI's human resources unit. There are many challenges. Within the Orang Rimba communities the child mortality rate is almost fifty percent. It is clear that traditional knowledge is unable to cope with an increasing variety of old and new diseases.

I think about the process of cultural change. On one hand, the Orang Rimba accept goods given to them by the outside world. On the other hand, they reject the underlying values and the way of life associated with those goods. Even when the Orang Rimba accept modern products, there is resistance and a gap emerges between the new attitudes and traditional knowledge. This is how the process of fusion normally takes place. Every change becomes a catalyst for the next change. However, it is not a predictable process. Consequently, when focusing on the issue of the Orang Rimba's wellbeing, there is a need to think broadly and holistically across many areas, including not just health and education, but their whole way of life in the rainforest.

May 24, 2000
Going home again

I am waiting for my ride back home. They are going to pick up my colleagues first, on the other side of Bukit Dua Belas National Park, so their arrival time is unpredictable. I have packed everything into my bag. The children are working on their last assignment on the small writing board. Every once in a while they furtively glance at me with sad expressions, but I pretend to be busy. I will be happy if the transport arrives late. We go through the same pattern every month when the children find out that I am leaving. We hardly speak for the whole day. Although my heart is with them, I have my next scheduled assignments waiting for me in the office. So, I pretend to ignore them. I take my notebook and reflect on my activities over the past seventeen days in the field.

I have twelve participants in this study program: Linca, Lemago, Pelesir, Besudu, Temiyang, Batu, Berenoy, Gentar, Miti, Ngelambu, Gemeram, and Ejam. The sessions have lasted effectively for fourteen days, from May 11-24, 2000.

Several drawbacks cloud the joy of my activities; these come primarily from the parents, but are aggravated by the slanderous influence of the timber merchants. I begin to ponder seriously the challenge of developing future Orang Rimba educational programs. Fundamentally, I have to understand the future underlying goals or reasons for our programs. I also realize that I need to bring these issues up during our monthly workshop and defend my findings in the field.

Let's postulate a theory, as clever people generally do.

The goal of education

Until now I have not defined an optimum education level for the Orang Rimba that satisfies the WARSI program objectives. Neither have I clearly thought about the context of my role as a facilitator of education. This month alone, at least five people have followed the education program, with better than expected results. So what will be the long-term follow-up?

I try to formulate the basic requirements for an Orang Rimba education program:

1. *Lessons need to be tailored to the Orang Rimba's daily activities.*
   Education materials need to be relevant to their needs and way of life. The materials also need to be designed appropriately to take into account the comprehension levels of the Orang Rimba.

2. *The Orang Rimba need to receive some benefit from any education program.*
   It is important that the Orang Rimba themselves recognize the benefits of education. I recall some advice from Parsudi Suparlan, the Dean of Anthropology at the University of Indonesia. He is regarded by some as headstrong, yet he is known to be very pragmatic. He said that any program seeking to re-direct a certain community outlook would not succeed if the people it is seeking to help do not share the belief that change is beneficial to them. Thus, any program benefits have to far exceed the negative spillover resulting from the acceptance of the change. It is also important that these benefits are maintained into the future and are open to revision when necessary.

3. *The education process needs to be locally organized.*
   The involvement of local people, bringing their language, local perceptions and culture into the mix, is likely to aid learning. Total integration by the teacher into the life of the Orang Rimba, with intermittent time outside the community, would contribute profound insights into any perception gaps between the two worlds.

4. *The education program needs to facilitate critical analytic skills and provide skills to assist the community in coping with the development challenges ahead.*
   There is a need for critical analytic skills to deal effectively with development and environmental changes. Development plans need to be explained in a transparent and honest way to each decision-maker and the inherent risks, which might affect their lives, need to be made apparent.

5. *The basic goal of any education program includes facilitating the Orang Rimba's capacity for self-realization, providing a vision for the future and developing self-integrity within the Rimba community.*
    Education programs should be aimed toward preparing the Orang Rimba to fend off external pressure, thus enabling them to master their own future direction.

This is roughly what I plan to write in my report. There it is, ladies and gentlemen, our lecture for today.

"Honk! Honk!" Ah, the unwelcome transport finally makes its way to us, snatching me away in front of the children who have been working so enthusiastically these last few days.

I leave. There is no waving of hands because this gesture is not part of the custom of the Orang Rimba. They say goodbye with glazed eyes. This sure ain't easy. Can I go through this every month?

God, I love them. The Orang Rimba, these unusual people.

Chapter 7

Does School Bring Bad Luck?

July 6, 2000
The fall of the steel wall

I felt like I had been struck by lightning when I heard that *Temenggung* Bedinding Besi had died on June 28, 2000. *Bedinding* (wall) and *Besi* (steel) truly describe this man. Not long after that, his daughter, *Indok* Ngerepal, who was nine months pregnant, died. One week later, the daughter of *Indok* Ngerepal, an unnamed girl aged five, also died. Another child had died in early June. Within the span of three weeks, this group had lost five of its members.

These deaths called for a significant *melangun*. In this case, the Orang Rimba had to journey to a distant place. They started from the palm oil plantation and travelled in an easterly direction from the Transmigration Unit, entered Kasang Panjang, continued to the Makekal River and Sungkay alongside the Tabir River, then to Lancar Tiang and the Kejasung Besar River. From here they planned to continue to the Kejasung Kecil River until they reached Serenggam. If this route were measured in a straight line from start to finish, it would be 40 km long. This distance disguises the difficulty of the journey. Much of the route is located in steep and mountainous terrain and there are large areas of swampy ground to traverse.

July 7, 2000
Does Sokola bring calamity?

Gentar is the only student who arrives this morning. We exchange news about what has been happening over the past two weeks in the rainforest while I was in Bangko. Gentar recounts spine-chilling stories and I have difficulty believing them. He says that the village people have put a magic spell on the *Temenggung* Bedinding Besi group with serious witchcraft like *tuju gembung* hexes. He says that if outsiders try to interfere, they will be the next to be cursed. My skin crawls. Am I one of those people who interfered? After all, I have been told that I was meddling in their lives. Can they transform me into a frog or a floor mat?

Quite honestly, I cannot afford to be concerned about this gossip. My thoughts are with the members of the Orang Rimba at the Bedinding Besi *rombong*. They must be heartbroken to have lost their leader. I especially want to know how my students are doing because I am quite attached to them now.

"Let's go and find them," I say resolutely. Gentar looks at me unconvinced. He doesn't want to go. Then he answers in a trembling voice, "Really? Can we go there?" I see a flicker of hope in his eyes.

We ready ourselves for the trip, buying this and that. We make sure to bring only essentials and some small gifts, such as non-perishable foods. These are intended as a goodwill gesture, to give to the grieving family during the *melangun* ritual.

July 8-9, 2000
Visit by a bear

We decide to follow the same route the *rombong* Bedinding Besi took for their *melangun*. *Ibu* and *Bapak* Pariyan try several times to discourage us from our plan. They say it is dangerous. I am puzzled. I think things have been dangerous all along, what has changed? However, I keep quiet. I reason with *Ibu* Pariyan that according to Orang Rimba custom, it is only natural for friends to visit and express their condolences to those in mourning. *Ibu* Pariyan stops making comments and accepts my determination to go. She accompanies us grimly to the end of the road and remains there standing, gazing, until we disappear behind the eclipsed shadows of palm plantation and jungle. I clutch a parcel of rice and other food she has given to us. It will do nicely for lunch. We walk away in silence. I try to lighten the mood by telling jokes, but Gentar refuses to laugh. I agree. There is nothing funny about this journey.

What Gentar said the day before still rings in my ears, "They will not like it, *Ibu*; they will send us back as soon as they see us, Bu. They say they are cursed because of you." I said, "In that case we have to tell them it is not true." Gentar sighed, unconvinced. "We have to see them!" I insisted.

I dislike walking under the palm trees, the sun seeps between the leaves and the air is stifling, musty and humid. I feel quite depressed.

103

Palm oil plantations are often infested with snakes, so we need to be cautious and ready to strike with a machete at a moment's notice. After two hours of walking on the northern side of the plantation, we begin to enter an area of rainforest that has been cleared for cultivation. Another kilometer in and we enter a devastated rainforest. All the trees have been felled and mutilated by wailing chainsaws.

At around two o'clock, we encounter some loggers. Several of them begin to utter vulgar and rude words in a *Batak* dialect. Apparently, according to Gentar, I am known in these parts as the *Batak* girl who seeks death. I stay quiet but walk with a furrowed forehead. I am frightened as well as irritated. Quietly I say to myself, "Say what you like. But I dare you to approach, if you do I will cut your head off!"

Later in our journey, we come across some working buffalo. Gentar tells me how much he hates the buffalo that haul logs to trucks and wood depots at the edge of the river. The logs are then floated downstream during the rainy season. I think he means that he hates the people who involve the buffalo in clearing the rainforest. Gentar continues to explain. He actually pities the animals that are essentially enslaved for the sole purpose of carrying logs. I tend to agree with him because I have witnessed how often the men beat the animals with huge wooden clubs. Gentar adds that he finds the buffalo repulsive and he is disinclined to help them. In Orang Rimba tradition, buffalo are regarded as taboo animals.

We continue walking towards the jungle leading us to the Tanagaro village by the Tabir River. It is now three o'clock and I am starting to feel hungry. Gentar once again instructs me to stay put while he explores the surrounding area. Meanwhile, I just sit and enjoy the ambience of the rainforest while the chattering birds, perched on their branches, look at me suspiciously. I open *Ibu* Pariyan's parcel of rice. I search for two wide leaves to serve as our plates and divide the rice between them. Gentar returns looking totally exhausted. He says his backpack is feeling heavier and heavier. We start eating, chatting about this and that. He says that he was in this area only six months ago but the roads have changed a lot and many new ones have been created. He seems to be perturbed and confused. It does not make much difference to me because everywhere we go in the jungle, I am totally lost anyway. To me, it seems equally confusing all around, and I have no notion of which path leads where.

After the late lunch, Gentar starts searching again. He finds something. There are signs of an Orang Rimba camp further away up the path among the thickets. We recognize it right away; the remains of an Orang Rimba camp are quite different from those of the village people.

We search for clues about which direction they have taken. At one campfire, we find shreds of torn paper. It looks like they have been torn on purpose, stamped on and then set alight. However, they are not completely burnt. I am shattered. The torn paper is from the books I had given them. Gentar stares at me. He then says that the parents must have found out about the books the children had been hiding. They blame schooling for bringing this curse from the gods, which caused the succession of deaths in the *rombong*.

I pick up the one piece that is still intact. We continue walking. We finally arrive at the mouth of the Makekal River and then go in the direction of the Tabir River. I am too frightened to look toward the Tanagaro village on the other side of the river. I'm afraid somebody might notice me and maybe want to kill me. Many people have expressed their hatred for me, for having influenced the Orang Rimba children to disobey their parents. They point to my stories about the sale of timber. I use these stories to explain the outside world. For example, I explain how outsiders purchase trees at a very low cost then sell the logs to others for the production of products of very high value.

We continue to walk upstream along the bank of the Tabir River. Soon we arrive at Lancar Tiang village. We walk past in a hurry. Some village people call out, but I do not stop. I try to smile and excuse myself politely. We then turn Southwest and follow the logging track, which is four meters wide and wedged between the rubber plantations. These muddy red earth tracks are always full of piles of stolen logs. The air is scorching hot. It feels like torture. I know I have to endure this torment for some time because there is still a long way to go. The distance from Lancar Tiang village to the log bridge over the Kejasung Godong River is around eight and a half kilometers. Uff . . . the air is full of mosquitoes too, like in any rubber plantation. Palm oil plantations are just full of snakes.

I begin to notice that Gentar is always on guard, he is watching over me. I realize that apart from the physical burden of carrying provisions and looking for directions, he also carries the moral responsibility of looking after me, all thanks to my stubbornness in roaming dense rainforests and visiting distant villages. We march on boldly, breathlessly. My clothes are now soaked and I am dripping with sweat. It won't be much longer, I think consolingly.

We turn left at the end of the track. I am out of breath. We have been walking now for more than eight hours. I begin to feel hunger pangs. It is also starting to get dark and I can hear the forest owl hooting at the moon as usual. "Let us stop *Ibu*," Gentar says. "Ah, it would be a pity, perhaps they are nearby," I say. "At night time, there is the risk of bears wandering around," replies Gentar. "In that case, we should continue until we cannot see the track anymore," I insist.

We start moving again. Suddenly out of the blue, the track disappears. Now we are lost. There is no path and no trace or mark. Gentar tells me to stop. He walks around a bit, looking for clues. Suddenly he stumbles on a piece of cotton thread caught on a low bush. Incredible! He says it is a strip of special wrapping cloth used by the Orang Rimba. He is sure of it. "To the right," he orders and we begin our march again.

Oh, this journey is exhilarating. It reminds me of an adventure story from my childhood, *The Lima Sekawan* or *The Famous Five* series of novels written by British author Enid Blyton. I used to imagine I was one of the "five"—four children and their dog solving a mystery while on school holiday. I daydream about a time when I only thought about climbing trees, sneaking through old castles, and escaping from criminals, all while using scientific theories to analyze the mystery set out before me. I smile to myself—how beautiful it would be if life were just about adventure, with no need to work or to buy things, time for adventures. All of a sudden the sky clouds over and it begins to drizzle. Gentar starts to speak loudly, perhaps annoyed by my stubbornness. "*Ibu*, now we must stop!! We need to find a good place to make a shelter. It is dark, plenty of bears and rain!" "*Au ... au ...*" I say, feeling guilty.

We walk slowly, keeping our eyes open for a good flat spot, protected from the rain and away from felled trees. But before we succeed, the skies open and the rain comes pouring down. We immediately undo the plastic covering sheet. Oh no . . . it is still in its roll; it has not been cut down the middle. We are frantic, trying to protect our backpacks and tent from the rain, using the uncut plastic sheet. By the time we manage to hook the plastic sheet to four corners posts, we are thoroughly drenched. We set up the tent. It is really practical for this sort of traveling, although I have never liked tents. One of the four poles is broken, so we make do with three and curl up inside the tent.

We are thoroughly soaked, itching all over, and starving. Gentar asks if he should cook, but I say no. I do not have the heart to ask him. Cooking would require the impossible task of finding wood which will not burn easily in these very wet conditions. Ah, there is even the risk of being attacked by a bear. I suggest we ease our hunger with crackers.

Gentar is so shattered he falls asleep squatting, holding several crackers in his hand. I am still awake, surrounded by a cacophony of peculiar noises. It does not take long for me to fall asleep, or more correctly doze off, Butet-style.

I awake to a really strange sound, "argh . . . . argh . . ." and scratching at our tent. It sounds like claws, I think. I hold tight to my machete in total silence. It does not occur to me that this is an animal sound. It is too weird, it must be the sound of a ghost, well, if ghosts exist. I sense the creature moving around our tent scratching here and there. The creature walks around for about five minutes, and then ambles away. I am still alert. Finally exhaustion wins over and I go back to sleep. Do what you want now, ghost! I am afraid, but I am going to sleep. I am just too tired to care!

In the morning, we are shocked to find many bear paw prints around our tent, and muddy claw marks on the wall of the tent. Apparently it was a bear, not a ghost. Lucky us, we were too scrawny for his liking.

We rush to pack and fold the tent. We do not want to stay around this area much longer. We continue our journey. About half an hour later, we emerge from the rainforest canopy to an opening overgrown with wild grass. Oh, the bright sun is blinding, and our eyes still half asleep. We have come to a fork. Gentar takes off in a flash, telling me to stay put. Darn it! Did he forget that a bear came to visit us last night? I stand on guard holding my big knife and searching for any reasonable tree to climb, just in case the bear reappears.

Gentar reappears after several minutes, having tracked down some signs. "Again?!" Ah, he is awesome, with uncanny Orang Rimba skills. These people could all be members of the Indonesian Army Special Forces! We enter the jungle again. An hour later we cross paths with a hunter, a member of the Linca *rombong* who gives directions to Gentar and we go our separate ways.

My heart is pounding. I have mixed feelings. *Aduh* . . . I feel the butterflies in my stomach, as if I am going to meet a lover. There is fear as well as tension. What do I fear? Am I afraid of being rejected by this group? Hmm . . . not exactly. My greatest fear is this: what if my pupils say to me, "Just leave, *Ibu*. Because of our studying with you, we were cursed by the gods." I begin to wonder as I look up to the sky through the rainforest canopy. "Divine Gods, whoever, whatever you are, is it true that my schooling brought on this curse?"

We are both feeling anxious and we walk faster. Gentar reminds me, "*Ibu*, they may kick us out. Can you accept that?" I just nod. "Yes, there's nothing I can do." I am resigned. At the very least, I have made the effort to meet them.

Suddenly, we hear something. Gentar signals me to be quiet. We peek through the leaves. Look! I see Temiyang. He has changed so much. He is thinner, darker, and looks exhausted. Like ghosts, we slowly show ourselves. He reacts right away. Taken by surprise, he shouts, "Eh?? My goodness. It is Bontet!!" He jumps up and down excitedly, and runs around. "Linca, Linca, my teacher is here!! You know, Bontet!" "Is it true?" Linca is stunned.

They both run toward me, jumping up and down, laughing. They look at me. Their eyes embrace me. I have the urge to hug them, but I have mixed feelings that I cannot identify. My wish has come true. I have truly missed them, as if they were my own children. Hah, what do I know, I don't even have any children! I surprise even myself.

Still, I am a woman and from a different world too. I have to respect their customs and cannot express my pleasure and hug them. In the end, I offer my hand. They are a little confused but shake my hand. I ruffle their hair. Excited, they behave as though they are young children, although they are in their teens. I forget that it is not their custom to shake hands. But if I make any gesture, they respond. I notice their eyes, like mine, are filled with tears of joy.

It is already dusk. We start to build our huts. I excuse myself while the boys continue building and helping with general cooking preparations. They also help me by preparing a cooking corner. I take some gifts out of the bag and look for *temenggung's* wife to express my condolences. I have brought rice, sugar and biscuits. After wandering among the huts, I find her curled up alone, below a *susudungon*, a little distance from another cluster of huts. She looks morose, her eyes are lifeless, gazing. She is whimpering, although no tears are apparent. That is the way of the Rimba. They cry when they feel sad, often without tears. When she catches sight of me, she howls and starts wailing, still without tears. I am perplexed but remain calm.

I rush over and she suddenly hollers, "Eee . . . my friend, *Bepak* has died . . . he has died . . . ."

I hug her, stroke her back, and without realizing it, I am in tears. It is still vivid in my mind how only a few weeks ago it was the husband who was sitting here, worried sick about his ill wife. Next to her then, the *temenggung* looked in great form. Such is the unpredictability of life.

"It's okay . . . Everything will be all right . . . be patient my friend," I try to console her.

Still sobbing in my arms, she opens the plastic gift-wrap, exploring the content and whispers, "Friend, did you bring some instant noodles?"

The question takes me by surprise. It is ironic, she still remembers *Supermi* (a popular brand of Indonesian instant noodles), even in her mourning. Hmm . . . must be her favorite food. *"Aduh,* I did not my friend."

The sobbing starts again, still without tears. I have the urge to laugh, but control myself as best I can.

"What about sardines?"

"Sorry . . . no sardines either".

This is dreadful. The wailing grows louder, still without tears. I try to comfort her. At the same time, I begin to feel irritated. How can craving food be more important than grieving for her husband? I withdraw, saying I am exhausted from carrying the rice, sugar, and biscuits for her. I plead with her not to ask for things that I do not have. She nods in a fluster.

I rejoin the children. Others begin to arrive, and we drown in the excitement of exchanging stories of events that have taken place since we last parted. We chill out on a four-by-five meter tarp spread out on the jungle floor. The boys and girls happily squeeze into the limited space. Despite the crammed space, we are quite comfortable. While sharing stories, we cook seaweed jelly for snacks.

Suddenly, a colony of *selembedo* ants attack me. It is excruciatingly painful. I jump up and down stamping and squashing them. The children are ecstatic joining in the fray in the best spirit of camaraderie. They tell me to move to the other side of the mat.

They pull aside the section with ants on it. The girls and I are told to stand at the other end and look the other way. Initially I am perplexed. It turns out that the boys have an effective way to handle the ants, by peeing on them as a group. Ah, ingenious!

We tell stories for two hours. Then, I bring out thin comic storybooks with pictures depicting a cat fighting a ball of cotton, ending up entangled and unable to move. There is also a story about a clever turtle that succeeded in winning a race with a deer. Gentar leads the reading and they all laugh together. Those children unable to read just stare vacantly at the books, and glance jealously at Gentar and the others. Their faces express a longing to understand the books beyond just a guess at the content from the pictures.

I move to a corner of the plastic mat, put down my mattress and cover myself with my sarong. I observe them quietly. Three children, who are unable to read, try to understand the words and create stories from the pictures. I smile, "Ah . . . how funny, I will teach you to read tomorrow!" Actually their stories are more charming than those in the book. The situation becomes funnier when they each recite their own version of the story. The more exciting the story, the more likely the others will listen. They grow animated and agitated with each other, as each believes their own interpretation. In the end, the most intense and exhilarating story is the version that everyone follows.

I lie down on my mat. My eyes drift to the darkening horizon and the sky above. How magnificent are those stars sprinkled above! I feel at one with these stars, their brilliance traveling from far and beyond. There are the sounds of birds, similar to the owl's hoot, and the chirping of crickets that salute each other in harmony. There are a host of other unknown musical participants out there in the dark. What a splendid night . . . .

It is almost eleven. Some children have fallen asleep on the books, possibly damaging them. Others fall asleep hugging their books. One child is awake, still turning the pages of a book, trying to fathom the incomprehensible letters, while snorting in the snot that had formed a number eleven under his nose. Occasionally, he wipes it with his loincloth, other times with his hand, and then he returns to turning the pages again. Ah . . . this is quite endearing.

I never get tired of looking at these children. I stare at the sky again. It has now become pitch dark and the stars are disappearing. Ah . . . I hope it won't rain on the twenty bodies sprawled on the ground under the open sky. I wonder what to expect the next day. I have not yet met the *Bepak*. I think about what Gentar has said, about maybe being kicked out. Oh . . . I give up. Tomorrow comes with its own agenda. The most important thing is that I have spent time with the children and know they are enjoying my visit. Now, it is time to sleep. My eyes begin to feel heavy. As always, I say my prayers before sleeping, to thank God for the blessings he gives me each day.

July 10, 2000
School during melangun

Yesterday, when I arrived at this *rombong*, I noted that the group has located themselves near the Sungkay River, a six-hour trek from TSM SP in Bernai. Today, they are on the move again, continuing their *melangun* procession further up the Kejasung Besar River.

Once I arrive at the new location the boys report on their educational progress. They bring books and pencils. Those who don't have any ask for them. Linca, Temiyang and Batu, the three most advanced students, have taught them. I find that it is easier to teach those who have been taught by Linca and his friends. Some children progress very quickly. It is almost as if they have been "conditioned" to spell. Many youngsters, including the young girls, know that *B* with *A* sounds as Ba. However, they have no clue how to write the letter *B* or *A*.

When learning to read and write, it is spelling that is the most important, yet most difficult, to teach because it requires a logical comprehension of the sound of each letter and an understanding of how these sounds function to create a word. I think that all the children in this camp would be capable of mastering reading and writing (without arithmetic) effectively within four weeks. That is, if they wish to, and if I am allowed. Psychologically, the children are in good spirits even though they are in the midst of a *melangun*. Meanwhile, I observe the elders; they are preoccupied with sorting out their inherited possessions or sobbing. I plan to stay with them a little longer, accompanying them on their *melangun* journey.

July 11, 2000
"Go away, Butet!"

Today, *Bepak* Bepiun subtly and politely suggests that I leave. He says that he does not want to risk anything happening to me in the middle of the rainforest, far from any settlement. He also fears being cursed with bad karma, known as *hukum sio-sio*. He will allow me to stay on for one or two days more before departing.

They plan to go deeper into the jungle and he doesn't want to be inconvenienced if anything should happen to me. I try to convince him that nothing will happen and, if it does, I will be able to overcome it. I plead that even if something does happen, although it would be very sad, it will be of no consequence to anyone. But he perseveres, talking about things that have nothing to do with me being here. In short, he is a broken record, playing the same song over and over again. Finally, I think perhaps I should leave. I promise to depart within two days.

I relate my conversation with *Bepak* Bepiun to Gentar. He defiantly says it is just an excuse. The elders don't like my presence there. They say they fear more deaths. They think "the school" brings bad luck. Oh, how stupid of me! I still do not understand the social dynamics of the Orang Rimba.

During the day, the children check their animal traps and carry material from one site to the next. Sometimes I join them. I am not as strong as they are. Just carrying *pemungkuy* a short distance is exhausting for me. One *pemungkuy* contains one hundred sarongs, weighing approximately 30-40 kilograms. Worse still, the shape of the sack makes it most uncomfortable to carry. Well, I guess I shouldn't expect it to be like a backpack. I soon find that I don't have the strength to do such work. At sunset, the children gather together and stay late into the night. However, I have exhausted myself with the day's work.

July 13, 2000
I say goodbye

On the day before I leave, we study until two o'clock in the morning. Even then, the children are not happy to stop. I continue until I fall asleep. They write me messages expressing their pleasure and their wish to continue learning. They ask, "When are you visiting us next?" Ah, so sweet. Why do their parents want me to go? I feel like knocking their heads one by one.

With the *melangun* taking priority, the learning at the *sokola* has to be postponed indefinitely. Fortunately, during the *melangun* near the TSM SP A the month before, I managed to enroll and teach a number of new students like Linca and Temiyang. They have achieved reasonably good levels of reading, writing and arithmetic. I promise the children if we can get a small number of students, and if my employer allows me, I will return.

July 14, 2005
Traveling with Gentar and Linca

I am pleased finally to be able to set up a school in the middle of the jungle, although it only lasts for four days. I really enjoy my time there, being in the midst of the children and in the middle of nowhere. I feel that the students are more carefree, enthusiastic, and obviously happy. They are completely uninhibited and without a care in the world. I have never encountered this atmosphere at the TSM.

Finally, I have to leave with a heavy heart. I do not know if, in the future, this pleasant, unique opportunity will ever come again. I hope it will.

I think about arranging a meeting with the Orang Rimba at Air Hitam. I suggest to Linca that he come with me to teach at Air Hitam, although at the back of my mind I have concerns about his parent's potential refusal. Linca is enthusiastic about the idea and brushes off my concerns. While it is true that neither of Linca's parents ever expressed their disapproval, other parents were dismayed that Linca would just take off like this with me. Temiyang, Linca's brother, kindly promises to leave signs at every fork in the trail, in case Linca wants to catch up with the group later.

The time finally arrives when Gentar, Linca and I must depart. The contrast between the two boys still amazes me. Each comes from a different group, and both are blessed with different innate abilities. Linca is more inclined toward writing, while Gentar is far more mathematical. They also possess contrasting personalities. Gentar is affectionate while Linca is mischievous. Since their time at school together, they have become great buddies and loyal friends. Initially, I was a little concerned about Linca's influence over Gentar. However, the opposite seems to have happened, with Gentar turning out to be dominant.

Once, Linca persuaded me to touch poisonous leaves, which would have made me itch, while Gentar shouted at me not to do it. Another time, Linca laughed out loud when he saw me fall off a bridge, while Gentar ran down into the creek to help me out. Yet, recently, Linca's "naughtiness" seems to have decreased.

July 16, 2000
Chasing Trainees?

We left Kejasung Besar two days ago and as we travel, the three of us chat and study together. During the journey, I give the two boys the next level of reading material. I have had some difficulty creating appropriate teaching method to use to teach them to read. Finally, I decide to use material written in long hand for reading practice. I also introduce them to official letters such as invitations and contracts. For contracts, I use the territorial agreements between the village people and Orang Rimba, paying attention to tone and punctuation. For invitation letters, I pay particular attention to the address and the date the letter was issued. We also focus on details such as the time, place and topic of the letter. Equally important is the formatting and the size of the lettering. Last, we cover salutations, closing sentences, and the signature of the sender as proof of identity.

I teach them to write stories and rhymes. In particular, I point out that rhyme may be written 'backwards' because of the need to match the final sound of each line. In contrast to legends or stories written in paragraph form, rhymes should be easy to read and understand. I am impressed by one story written by Linca. I like it because it is very humorous and one can easily visualize this happening with the Orang Rimba. It goes like this:

A Fairytale about *Bepak* Andi
by Linca

Ado Bepak Andi masang jorot Kijang baru ditingoknye turuy ditangkopnya Kijang itu baru diikatnya Kijang pada kayu pakoy simpur miyang, baru digendongnya piado telap. Bepak Andi pikir, "Niyo ma, kijang godong nihan, mungkin akeh minta bini keh bentu ngundo." Bepak Andi pulang pado bininye. "Jorot akeh keno Kijang, akeh hopi telap ngundonye." Bininye nurut Bepak Andi. Nye koli baru nye tetawoko "Ha . . . ha . . ." bininye lepay tali baru diundonye Kijang itu "Bepak Andi lolo!" ujinye.

One day, a Rimba man called *Bepak* Andi set up a rope to trap a deer. He succeeded, got hold of the deer and tied it to a tree using a *simpur miyang* rope. Afterwards he tried to lift and carry the deer but it was too heavy for him. *Pak* Andi thought, "This deer is too big, I will ask my wife to help me carry it." He went home to his wife and said to her, "I trapped a deer, but I am not strong enough to carry it." The wife followed him. When she saw the deer, she burst out laughing. "Ha, ha, ha," laughed the wife. She loosened the rope that tied the deer to the tree and just walked the deer back home. "Stupid *Bepak* Andi!" she said.

A written piece by Gentar is also pleasant. This is an example of a *Pantun*, a traditional poetic form.

"In Solitude"
by Gentar

Koin panjang dua serentang
Dibawa numbuk padi begenti ari
Mano elok itu dipakay

Kalu buruk kami tukang menyepi

I have on hand, two lengths of cloth,
Both of them used for thrashing rice,
The one I'd use is the one most nice,
The other I'd store with balls for moths.

Like all *pantun*, this one carries a lesson. Gentar wants to convey his advice on how to choose a friend. The cloths represent two people and Gentar advises his reader to think carefully when choosing a friend; pick the one who keeps his word and ignore the one who breaks his promises.

They also write down incantations they know by heart. They know spells to use when stung by a millipede or scorpion. They say they will ask their parents for other spells as well as for Rimba customary laws, to memorize them and eventually write them down. They also express their regret at having missed the opportunity to learn various bits of knowledge from the late *Temenggung* Bedinding Besi, who had passed away.

During the time I am with them, I notice how clever these two boys are. Lately, I have been wondering whether they are not just clever but really at the genius level. Within this short span of five days, they are able to absorb and master material normally intended for at least two weeks of intensive teaching.

Apart from being astonished by their cleverness, I have to hold back my laughter sometimes. They can be so funny or silly. Actually, I am not sure whether it is their silliness or my ignorance. Just observe their logical thinking when given a math problem.

I am still unsure about how to teach addition. In the beginning, it was only necessary to explain the logic of adding numbers. However, the extraordinary answers they come up with take me by surprise.

$$\begin{array}{r} 18 \\ +25 \\ \hline 313 \end{array}$$

When I explain it is wrong, they insist, "*Ibu*, you said 8 + 5 is 13 right?"

If I dictate numbers to them and they write the sums down in their notebooks, the results are mind-boggling:

$$87$$
$$+\underline{145}$$
$$9115$$

They write from left to right, the same as when writing letters. I realize that I have not yet explained the logical concept of number placement and their groupings into tens, hundreds, and so on. Oh . . . how stupid I am. I realize my deficiencies from their mistakes.

They learned simple multiplication (for numbers less than ten) the month before, but nothing beyond that. They understand the processes and rules, although they have not quite mastered them. It is no wonder; they tackle multiplication by adding numbers together. This slows down the process.

For example, for them $7 \times 5 = 7+7+7+7+7=35$

I strongly urge the Orang Rimba to master multiplication. They initially resist, saying, "It's too complicated to remember multiplication tables. If it is similar to addition, we'll just use addition. We are not in a hurry; we can always just add." They explain that if they want to buy 5 kg of sugar and each kg costs Rp. 2,000, they can just add 2,000 + 2,000 + 2,000 + 2,000 + 2,000 to get Rp. 10,000.

So, I give them some difficult problems to solve. How much would it cost if each of the 54 people in your *gank* buys 5 kilos of sugar? What if each Orang Rimba, all 2,500 people, has 100 fleas? They use up many pieces of paper trying to write "100" twenty-five hundred times. They can't keep count of how many times they have written 100. I smile at my victory. Often I tease them "Give up? Come on, learn multiplication!" They shake their heads and try to ignore me while they keep counting. After sometime they give up and say, "Look, I think you are right, we need to learn multiplication!"

The Orang Rimba are very pragmatic. If they don't experience something for themselves, they will not easily believe me. I need to prove that something is useful before I teach it to them. Multiplication is important. It is essential in their day-to-day lives. For the time being, I let them copy and memorize the multiplication tables up to ten. They also start to do more complex problems.

279	321	781
x 7	x 20	x 187
1,953	000	5467
	642	6248
	6,420	781
		146,047

I summarize the rules:

1. There are only two factors in multiplication.
2. The top number to be multiplied is called the factor, and the bottom one is called the multiplier.
3. The factor is multiplied by the multiplier (bottom), in strict order from the end number on the right (units, tens, hundreds, etc.)
4. The result of this multiplication is written below the line. The next step is recorded below the previous result, leaving a space on the left.
5. The end result of multiplication is derived by totaling these numbers.

Is it right or wrong to use children for experimentation? Sometimes I feel guilty using the Rimba children as the testing ground for my ideas. Other times I am excited. It is as if we have new toys every day, new things to test and to play with.

I also begin to combine arithmetic and problem solving. In Rimba daily life, multiplication is critical for dealings with the outside world. For example, to sell rubber: y kg. of rubber at a price per kg. of z, for a total price of y x z. Also, for instance, to sell land per square meter, it is crucial for the Rimba to comprehend the situation and to be able to translate it into a mathematical context.

I also stimulate their logic by using hypothetical situations:

> If a family has twelve *tano* (100 m²) and a rubber tree is planted every two square meters, and each rubber tree produces 2 ounces of rubber per day, what is the total amount of rubber produced? And, if the monthly total is divided equally among each member of the family, how much rubber would each member receive?

They are so excited, because the concepts of mathematics, of multiplication, addition and division now come into play in problems from their daily life. Once, I raised a similar daily life problem with the students in the village and they had no idea how to set up the calculation. I realize now, that even when I was in school in Jakarta, I wasn't taught to practice math that was practical for understanding my daily activities.

When it comes to division, especially using decimals and fractions, they again question the practicality of the math. I say, "When you have one durian to share among five people, each person will get 1/5th." They all of sudden laugh out loud, "Don't be silly, *Ibu*, each person gets one piece!" Hmm, I think, that is not a good example. I try again, "Ok, now I have one cookie. If I share it with five children, how much each will each child get?" As I break up the cookie, I am sure they will say 1/5th. And the answer is "Each child still gets one piece, *Ibu*! It's just smaller!!" Oh God, I give up! (Note: I was not able to convince them to learn fractions until 2009!)

They also ask to be taught how to tell time. I cannot fathom why the concept of time is so important to them. They bring me calendars from the market, some printed on the cover of notebooks, some with sexy women representing each month. They want to know what October means, or 1999 or 2000 or even Thursday. They know that Monday is market day, but Tuesday, Thursday and Saturday are days they have never heard of. I learn later that days and dates are important for them because they need to coordinate time with the outside world when they have a meeting or other administrative matter.

While explaining these concepts, I ask many questions about how the Orang Rimba keep track of time. The adage "as you teach so shall you learn" rings true for me. While doing so, I learn a lot about the cosmology of the Orang Rimba and how time is related to signs in the environment surrounding them.

Today is *Sari niyo*.
Tomorrow is *Isuk*.
The day after tomorrow is *Tekiyun isuk/Brenti isuk*.
Two days after tomorrow is *Tulatta*.
Yesterday is *Kamaria*.
The day before yesterday is *Basaariya*.
Two days before yesterday is *Sebelik Basaariya*.

Coincidentally, time for the Rimba tallies exactly with the seven-day week concept, just like with market day that repeats itself every seven days. Although here, market day is Monday, while for the Orang Rimba in another area it is always on Tuesday.

The timing of their month relies upon the appearance of the moon. Consequently, their month is shorter than one month in the outside world. They base their year on the appearance of fruit like durian or the start of honey season.

They actually do not really care about computing their age. This calculation often arrives at an interesting conclusion. I once asked a boy (about 15-17 years old) how old he was. His father answered, "Who knows? Let me count. He has experienced durian season 35 times. So, he must be 35 years old!"

When they cite a specific year, they make comparisons to historical or eventful times. For example, for the year 1998, they say a year after the "smoky winds". In fact, this was the year after there were many forest fires in Sumatra and the sky was full of smoke and haze.

It is also interesting to hear how the Rimba refer to hours in their daily life. The division of their time, compared to our 24 hours, is based on sounds and sights within their natural habitat. For example for 6:30 am, the Orang Rimba say *"butebut buit"* meaning when the *butebut* birds begin to sing. 3 pm to 6 pm is *"puang nyimpoy"* meaning when the sun starts hiding—in the jungle the sun hides behind the trees by three and sets by six. Eight o'clock in the evening is *"tidur budak"* (children's sleeping time), and 10 to 11 pm is *"tidur rerayo"* (parents' sleeping time).

I introduce them to points of orientation in the environment, connecting them to maps and specific points or places in the outside world. In their daily life the Orang Rimba use directions such as upstream or downstream, using a river as a benchmark. For North, they use the village of Tanagaro, located in the north, as an orientation point. Likewise, Air Hitam is used to point South. To explain the general concepts of maps, I stress that North is the top portion, and I describe the map's legend and the idea of scale. I also explain how a compass works, and how it always points North. By chance, I have a compass with me, although it is a little small. It is as small as a marble, so many heads bump trying to see it.

Chapter 8

Suddenly Teachers

July 17, 2000
My two geniuses

Gentar and Linca, my two geniuses, are very motivated. They know I want them to teach elsewhere. Occasionally, they express their frustration, lamenting that they are still inadequately prepared but, at the same time, they ask for reassurance.

"*Ibu*, am I clever enough now?"

"Ah, I am still stupid, eh? Or am I smart now?"

"Am I capable of teaching others?"

I explain to them, that in teaching, the way lessons are taught is more important than how the lesson plan is constructed. I emphasize the importance of having empathy and patience toward students and that these qualities can be demonstrated through behavior and words while teaching. I think back to when I was a student and I remember how important it was to have an amiable teacher who made learning fun. When I was in junior high, I always looked forward to my English class because I liked the teacher. Lessons that I used to hate with my former, boring teacher became my favorites and the time passed very quickly with an interesting teacher. I want to be that likeable teacher, not a monster everyone fears.

I think about the teachers I have had. I remember one time when some students cursed their teacher, wanting her to get diarrhea and not come to class. Other students ignored a teacher, leaving him talking endlessly like a broken record. I think of students who look at their teacher with blank expressions, their minds on a different planet, daydreaming about the pretty girl in class or the food in the cafeteria and pocket money for snacks, or those who simply stare pathetically. Oh, how sad to be that teacher! I would rather not be a teacher at all than be an unwanted teacher. And, I am a little worried I might experience "karma"—I used to laugh the loudest when a cursed teacher didn't show up for class.

This reminds me of a mean teacher I had in junior high. During a lesson, a friend of mine slipped me a drawing of the teacher tied to a tree and a person dressed in a bear suit poised ready for attack. The teacher was depicted peeing in his pants out of terror. This made me laugh out loud and the teacher called my name. I didn't hear him the first time, but the second time he called, the class went silent. Sure enough, I was almost hit by a blackboard eraser that zoomed past my head like a jet plane. Good thing I was agile and he missed. Then, I was kicked out of class. Outside, I smiled at myself, cursing my friend, the cartoonist. Fortunately, I had hidden the picture in my desk drawer, so the teacher was unable to find the reason for my laughter. The next day, I was summoned to his office. He said that he thought I might be insane because of my spontaneous and loud laughter in class. He added, "You really should see a psychiatrist!"

I advise Gentar and Linca on the nature of teaching. I counsel them to involve themselves with their students, by collecting wood or sharing the cooking, by checking animal traps or hunting. I suggest that they try to be flexible and make friends with their students. As a teacher, it is important to be aware of your students' moods. Do they lack concentration? Are they bored or tired? Does their body language show that they are in another place? Are they tapping their fingers, sighing heavily or yawning? If so, you should stop teaching immediately!

Naturally, the community purpose of education and why it is important for the Orang Rimba at this time overrides all these considerations for the students. Knowledge of the benefits of education should be their motivating spirit, ingrained in their souls, wherever they go in the jungle. It should not be difficult. They already had the seed of this idea before they started learning with me. Obviously, this is the engine that drives them to want to learn, despite opposition from their parents. It also has become clear that pressure from the outside world cannot be overcome through customary Rimba traditions. The Orang Rimba need more tools.

I ask them if they are ready to start. The funny thing is that their concerns are elsewhere. They say, "We are worried about being fined by the chief of WARSI for traveling with a woman." Of course, I am this "woman". They ask repeatedly if there are any laws governing fines for men who travel with women (who are not their sisters or cousins). After I explain that there are no restrictions, they feel reassured.

121

I train them in the main tasks of being a teacher, experimenting with different methods of teaching and working with a progressive order of lessons. They take turns practicing in front of the blackboard. They have excellent memories, and they impersonate me in everything I do, down to the most minute detail. For example:

"The letter H is like a rope for hanging laundry and it sounds like you are sleepy," they say, yawning.

"The letter M has three legs. Say it with closed lips, and make a long sound mmmmmm," they say pointing to their lips and raising their eyebrows.

"When pronouncing the letter M by closing the nose, the sound will not come out, and it's called a nasal sound!"

They explain all the letters and numbers quite well, impersonating me perfectly. I find it quite funny. In the process of watching them teach, I see myself and realize that the way I teach must indeed look a bit funny. I can also see areas where I can improve my teaching style.

July 18, 2000
Literacy infantry is on the move

"Are we actually sitting down while running?" Linca asks when we ride in WARSI's jeep on our way to Air Hitam. We all laugh. Gentar sits in front next to the driver, and I am in the back with the backpacks.

Linca turns around to face the back seat and says, "In this position, it is called running in reverse, yes?"

Aduh, so original! I would love to clone them. They are such good entertainment for me . . . he he he.

Ah, I am watching my impossible wish come true. I am taking my best, three-month-old students to other locations to "suddenly become teachers"—the accidental teachers.

Our jeep moves swiftly past the last transmigration village and palm oil plantation, until finally we arrive at an embankment at the edge of the rainforest. The Orang Rimba call this embankment Bendungan Punti Kayu. We get out and start to re-pack, throwing away anything that might slow us down on the journey. We know that ineffective packing can increase our travel time from three to five hours.

Heading to Rombong Kedundung Muda

We begin our journey by crossing over the top of a dam right behind the water gates. It is quite slippery. If we slip and fall, at the very least we end up with black-and-blue bottoms. Of course, if we land bottom first we are lucky, but imagine if we land headfirst? I don't like to think about that.

The rainforest we just passed through was heavily deforested. It has been completely planted with the villager's crops. Some patches belong to the Orang Rimba, an attempt to confine the encroachment of village crops. Having never been here before, we just guess our way.

It is already past one o'clock when we come to a river with a tree trunk serving as a bridge. The trunk is small, with a diameter of less than 15 centimeters. It is very slippery with the muddy footprints left by other Orang Rimba. I have successfully crossed three bridges like this, but only with the encouragement of both Gentar and Linca. I don't need someone to hold my hand; I only ask them to be ready to catch me if I slip and fall. Thankfully, they carry my backpack across so I can concentrate on crossing the bridge.

I imagine that our group must look strange compared to others entering the Rimba. The loggers lug chainsaws, machetes and sacks of rice while the farmers bring spades or hoes. Well, we carry a writing board the size of a backpack, dangling from the back of Linca's bag. The pack has a peculiar shape. Inside are books, chalk and other writing materials. We also bring two posters of letters and numbers. Linca seizes any opportunity for a break. He grabs the small writing board and asks me to test him on a variety of problems. He even keeps a piece of chalk in his pocket.

By sunset, we arrive and meet Nggrip. I am not sure whether we were slow or had simply made too many stops. My watch shows that it is past six o'clock in the evening. Fortunately, darkness comes later here. Still, for the last 10 minutes of the journey, we were walking in the shadow of darkness.

With each step in the rainforest I am filled with uneasiness. I remember meeting Nggrip earlier, when he expressed dislike for having Orang Rimba from other groups come to teach his people. He much preferred being taught by *Orang Luar* (people from outside). I never mentioned this to Gentar and Linca. I presume it is a question of "face", that it is embarrassing to be taught by their own kind from a different group. Indirectly, it might be perceived as an admission that the other group is somehow superior.

I brush off my fears. I figure that I do not have the strength or capacity to teach everybody. At most, I can teach about ten people at a time. A larger class is too difficult to supervise, and there are times when I need to teach one on one.

Much to my relief, Nggrip shows no sign of hostility when he sees my young Orang Rimba assistants. He is enthusiastic to get everything ready.

There are six children who always study with me: Pengusai, Beseling, Mulung, Gemambun, Mendawai and Nggrip. Based on a report I read in the office, they are students of the late Yusak. This group was the last to welcome him before he died of malaria. Yusak had started teaching them the alphabet. Like me, he had difficulty teaching them to spell by joining individual letters. As I become familiar with the students, I find that they retain the alphabet well. Nearly all of them identify letters correctly, but stumble when combining them in spelling tasks.

I am taken aback with the small number of pupils. When I met Nggrip in Bangko, he recommended 30 potential pupils, twelve who were more than eight years old. This is why I brought my two trainees. A little investigation reveals that the group has split due to some "quiet" disagreements. The group is now divided into three *rombong*: *Bepak* Meratai, *Temenggung* Nggrip and *Bepak* Bedoring. *Bepak* Meratai is the oldest leader; he must be in his seventies. He has seven children and Nggrip is his second son. *Bepak* Bedoring is *Bepak* Meratai's son-in-law. The three *rombong* have dispersed and are living in different places about a 20-minute walk apart. They normally gather at *Bepak* Meratai's place every afternoon, chatting and having coffee until night falls or the time for night hunting comes. After some discussion, we decide to stay with the *Bepak* Meratai group because they have more people and more potential pupils.

July 19, 2000
A very supportive rombong

Robert, from WARSI, is here coincidentally on an anthropological assignment. He helps us set up *Sokola Rimba*, we call it the Jungle School. He knows the Orang Rimba quite well and consequently, his presence is very helpful to us. The *sokola* plan is submitted directly to the elders.

Tengganai Bepak Meratai, the oldest and most respected person, gathers all the children and urges them to think about their future and the benefits of an education. The talk is informative. There are no suggestions, prohibitions or orders. Everyone is free to meet with me as they please. Ah, what a wise man. This is such a contrast to the other parents I have met elsewhere in this Rimba.

July 20, 2000
Gentar and Linca in action

The following day, I ask three people from neighboring huts if they are interested in attending the *sokola*. They agree eagerly. They say that *Temenggung* Nggrip spoke with them before we arrived.

This time, we only have eight days effectively, nine counting the day of our departure. It is a bit too short for us to develop relationships, but it is better than nothing. Most of the children are timid and afraid, especially of me. However, they get on well with Gentar and Linca almost immediately.

Depending on whom they are more comfortable with, they choose their own teacher. I pop in every once in a while during lessons, either helping to explain or reminding Linca and Gentar of missing information. I try not to stay with them too long because they become timid and self-conscious. Most of the time, I act cool and indifferent so they aren't distracted. I try my best to enjoy my time, all the while planning flexible and spontaneous 'home-made' curriculum materials and lessons.

July 21, 2000
Overconfident student

Today, an older man comes around carrying his own book and pen; he had bought them himself. He calls out, asking Gentar to teach him. He motions to Gentar to come and sit under a tree quite a long way away from us, warns us to not disturb their lesson or try to eavesdrop. How strange, I think. It turns out that he had previously told Robert that he did not want to be taught by Rimba children. According to him, Rimba children do not make good teachers. Also, he, like the other older men, did not want me to teach him. The pretext is that by having another teacher, a male teacher, they can maintain their respect for me.

This gender issue is a bit difficult for me to understand. It is not that the Orang Rimba men do not wish to have a woman as a teacher; they are worried that they will somehow disrespect me if I teach them. For the Orang Rimba, it is rude for a man to stare at a woman, and any woman who puts herself in a position to be stared at, well, she is considered disreputable. The older men feel badly that it might appear that they disrespect me and want to allow me to remain in a respectful position.

Subsequently, the man asks Robert to teach him. Robert rejects him outright, claiming that he does not have any talent as a teacher. Although Robert has taken courses at the Teaching Institute, he gave up teaching because he finds it difficult to be patient. During the training, he hit an errant junior high school student, and the enraged parents went to the schoolmaster. The schoolmaster gave Robert a warning, and Robert realized that teaching was not his path, preferring to be an anthropologist.

Robert tells the man, "If you are willing to be punched every time you make a mistake, then I will teach you!" The student responds right away. "Whoa there! There is no way I am willing to let you do that!"

Fortunately, the man 'lowers his expectations' and is happy to be taught by Gentar and sometimes Linca. Nevertheless, Linca complains a lot, saying he is a very difficult student. Meanwhile, Gentar takes it in his stride and tolerates having this somewhat eccentric student. As is often the case, the older man fears losing face if corrected by a child.

It is quite comical to watch this man copy all the words from Gentar's book, then declare that he knows how to read and write. He puts a lot of effort into meticulously copying the words, and he asks Gentar how to read them. Then, he tries to memorize the words, a series that reads BATU (stone), RUSA (deer), LIMA (five). He proudly demonstrates his "reading" ability to us, repeating the words he has simply memorized. "*Ibu*, this reads BUKU (book), this one reads RUSA." I just grin. I ask Gentar to explain to him that this repetition of sounds does not mean he is reading. Gentar, in protest, complains that he has done so many times and, in return, *Bepak* reprimands him with verbal insults. Ah, poor Gentar.

July 27, 2000
Different groups, different motivation

The students at *rombong* Kedundung Muda seem to be slower than those in Gentar and Linca's group. By comparison, they achieve in eight days what Linca's group achieved in two or three. They are only at the level of memorizing the alphabet and using a basic form of the spelling and reading system. At this stage, they use simple vowel/consonant letter combinations (BA-BI-BU-BE-BO to YA-YI-YU-YE-YO). Then, they progress to two syllable consonant/vowel patterns such as *bebi, buku, madu,* and *demo*.

The contrast between these two groups is striking. Linca's group are diligent, pro-active, and quick and have higher levels of concentration.

They study under pressure, defying the belief that school is taboo. This pressure might be the reason they perform better.

Linca and Gentar's groups are happier and more cheerful when studying. They seem addicted to their education, always impatient for it to start. They rarely respond yes when I ask them if they are tired of learning. They even request more work and compete among themselves to finish it, without ever trying to copy their friends' work. Often, they learn from those who have already acquired the skill and happy to oblige. They also focus on comprehension rather than grades. What a pleasant and progressive bunch.

In contrast, the children here tend to be passive, slow, easily tired, bored and less attentive. They lack curiosity and are sluggish. They often complain, "I am tired" or "Eee . . . I want to sleep" and then they lie down without permission.

In retrospect, the capacity to recall and the speed of memorization between the two groups is about equal. It is just that the class dynamics and student performance are, for some reason, significantly different when comparing results between Gentar and Linca's groups and the students in this *rombong*.

Another stark difference between the two groups is their motivation. Almost everyone in Linca's group wants to get an education. Some students are a little concerned about their parents' disapproval. However, these same children seem even more determined to learn. Other children discreetly take up studying from those already taught by me. This is the irony. The parents of this group encourage and approve of their children's study, but is it at a possible cost?

Another unique thing about the this group is that a few older men, having finished their search for rattan or work in the fields, come to watch our school every afternoon. They listen to our lessons attentively, nodding their heads when we explain things. Interestingly, they scold their children if they laze around or yell at them when they answer incorrectly. They press and encourage their children to study more seriously, especially since they know that our time with them is limited. Another opportunity may not come around for a few weeks, perhaps in the following month and this, too, is dependent on WARSI's approval.

July 28, 2000
Gentar and Linca

Gentar and Linca's readiness to be Orang Rimba teacher trainees in Air Hitam exceeds my expectations. They are even charming with the parents, introducing themselves with a warm familiarity. They still seek assurances from me with inquiring glances every now and then. I usually respond with a supportive expression.

Every night, we start a campfire and cook. We discuss and gossip about the children, as well as the adults. When there are enough children gathered, I encourage them to discuss the Orang Rimba customary ways. They discuss and debate issues among themselves. I am proud of them and cannot help smiling. The children who are knowledgeable about their customs earn the respect of their friends.

Whenever the children take a break from studying, Gentar and Linca continue their own studies; writing stories, reading novels, solving mathematical problems and simply occupying themselves with study. It is interesting to watch the children's faces—they are totally in awe of Linca and Gentar.

Occasionally, strong language slips out from Gentar or Linca when a student makes a mistake or is a little slow. They sometimes even yell at them. I never had the nerve to say such things. My response would be either to laugh, watching the student's completely vacant expression, or, if I couldn't stand it anymore, I might say, "Where is your knife? Why don't you just kill me?"

I remind Gentar and Linca not to reprimand students who make mistakes or are slow to learn. Nobody wants to make mistakes or wants to be called stupid. Despite the reminders, sometimes, they still lose their heads. I empathize with them because it is often the same mistakes over and over again. Strangely enough, the children do not seem to be offended or fed up, although I can't say they become more enthusiastic either.

Linca and Gentar teach with devotion. They have always been like this; from the first time they taught their friends at home. Their commitment shows no less here than it did with their own group. They are never stale, and do their best to maintain high levels of interest in class. Lessons pause only at the initiation of the students.

I find it hilarious to see Gentar's bewildered expression over the last few days. "*Ibu*, I think the wiring in my brain is getting fried from overheating!" he says while scratching his lice-ridden head.

Today, there are only three children studying. Gentar and Linca ask why there are so few students. I say, "It is not important. Later, these students can teach their friends. If there are too many, you might get a headache!" They answer, "Better to have a larger group because, regardless of their number, we still get a headache. The people here aren't fast learners." They also express their disappointment that the kids in this location are not enthusiastic about school, unlike the children from their own group.

Gentar and Linca negotiate with *Temenggung* Nggrip that, if he teaches them Orang Rimba law, in return both of them will teach the *temenggung* to read and write. It is a fair exchange.

Nggrip's comments make a strong impression on Gentar and Linca when they exchange stories on how the two groups perceive school so differently. "Whether or not there is a school, our natural habitat will be surely destroyed, so it is far better to have a school. If we are clever, people will not make fools of us. We can be rich. It would be good to have a house like the village people, and asphalt roads, to drive a car and watch TV."

Gentar and Linca get worked up over what Nggrip has just said and discuss it with me. Personally, I am afraid this approach might come back to hurt the Orang Rimba. The worst scenario would be if they actually sell their rainforest land to obtain money to establish a village.

When we return, both trainees are happy to find out they will be paid for their days spent teaching. I am not certain about whether this is correct. We had debated this matter in the office. Some colleagues suggested that they accept payment as pocket money. Others said depositing the money into a savings account would be better. Still others were concerned about the potential long-term financial impact of this precedent. Over time, for example, children's access to education might be limited by the teacher's need to be paid. The majority, however, agreed to compensate the boys for their effort and time spent. This is primarily because the time spent teaching is equivalent to or greater than time spent working as guides, from morning until late afternoon. Second, teaching takes a lot more effort for preparation, both mentally and physically. Third, their parents will not be happy if the boys return empty-handed. The children, on the other hand, unequivocally say they are happy to work without pay.

The current rate of payment is Rp. 17,500 per day, in line with a guide's fee. The real fee is actually Rp. 20,000, reduced to pay for food. I prefer to hand them the full amount. My daily allowance of Rp. 12,000 is sufficient to cover all our meals three times a day. Isn't that amazing? Well, we only have meals of rice with salted fried fish or a packet of instant noodles to share among three of us. Sometimes we make shrimp crackers, which turn soft in the humidity minutes after they come out of the frying pan.

Alas, what else is there to eat and drink here? Roast ham? Cocktails? It is not so much a matter of cost but rather a question of what we can carry and preserve. I design the meals so that I can carry a month's provisions. In an ideal world, there would be a small pill, which when doused with a drop of water, would transform itself into fried chicken. Or perhaps, a simple seed, when boiled, would mutate into a bowl of spinach big enough for Popeye. With these imaginary foods, it would be easy for us to carry all our food into the rainforest. It would be even better if the Orang Rimba would donate wild game to us. Now that would be perfect; it would be truly divine!

After reviewing our progress, it turns out that this current group has attained only one third of the level of educational achievement of Linca's group. In other words, it will take this group almost three times longer to arrive at the level achieved by Linca's *rombong*. Based on this, it will take approximately eighty school days for them to acquire basic reading-writing-arithmetic skills, or four monthly trips into the jungle. This same target was achieved in about twenty-eight days by Linca's group or just over two monthly visits.

This difference between the two groups is not my primary concern. I am more disturbed by *Temenggung* Nggrip's visions about future scenarios for the Orang Rimba. Nggrip is notorious for his unconventional methods, such as creating "permits" on plots of land for trees to be felled and selling forestry survey results. He also harbors a social ambition—to be considered an equal to the people in the village. He has taken steps in the past and now clearly demonstrates that he is all for "progress" among the Orang Rimba. He wants to be known as a modern, sophisticated person. He craves a motorbike or a four-wall house. These are highly valued because they demonstrate to others that he is a 'modern' man. However, his bombastic outbursts often bring disaster. Many times, the end result of his deals with outside people place the Orang Rimba in a worse position and deplete their natural resources further. He never seems to learn from his mistakes.

I get a headache thinking of the possible scenarios that could be the future destiny of the Orang Rimba, and the pain gets worse when I try to find sensible solutions.

Chapter 9

New Recruits

August 9, 2000
"You money-grubber!"

Ah, poor Gentar, he has to work by himself at Air Hitam because Linca joined his family on a *melangun* further upstream on the Kejasung Besar River. Gentar just discovered this when they were returning from teaching on the south side of the rainforest. Linca found the tracks of his family and said that he wanted to catch up with them.

Linca's *rombong* is trying to make their living by harvesting rattan. I also hear that some of my students are employed as loggers and are working with the Tanagaro village people. Linca has said that he wants to work as a rattan collector.

During my first three days in the rain, I stay along the Bernai River with the *Wakil* Tuha group. This is where Gentar lives. The main purpose of my visit is to fetch Gentar and bring him to teach at Air Hitam. I notice during my time here that this group's attitude toward education has improved. Miti, who joined us at the very beginning, wants to be assigned to Gentar. Three other boys, Anjur, Nyado and Sekodi also suddenly want to start school again. Their parents do not object, unlike before.

I suspect that this shifting interest in education is not borne out of a genuine desire for learning, but rather from the money they can earn by becoming teachers. They are pleased that Gentar has neither run away nor been kidnapped by the 'other world'. I find this mercenary attitude rather irritating, and so I reject Miti's offer to teach on the basis that he is not yet qualified. I also argue that we are still committed to teach at Air Hitam and thus cannot start a school at Bernai. It is neither Miti's fault nor that of his money-grubbing parents; I decide to stick to my principle of not including such people in the "traveling teacher" program.

Later, I realize that their focus on money shows that they are already part of the external economic system. The introduction of money into their society logically leads to a need to be more money-literate. From my anthropological studies, I understand that indigenous people often adopt aspects of modern life without being aware of possible detrimental consequences. For example, those who begin to wear clothes must learn how to wash them and those who begin to eat sugar must learn to brush their teeth.

I observe how rotten Orang Rimba teeth are, especially among those who live near villages and shop there, buying and consuming sugar and pre-packaged foods. Others suffer acne and dandruff. The Orang Rimba who either willingly join or are enticed to join the external economic system, often end up victimized. This is due to their ignorance of arithmetic, nutrition, and other things. Without basic literacy, they are easily deceived.

Therefore, the Orang Rimba in this particular area need immediate training. This is already an emergency situation!

August 13, 2000
Diligent Group

Today, Gentar and I visit *rombong* Kedundung Muda at Air Hitam. This *rombong*, especially their *Bepak*, could be described as one of the more industrious *rombong* when it comes to earning a living. Other Orang Rimba *rombong* are less entrepreneurial and tend to spend their days in a relaxed and easy manner.

The people in this *rombong* are always busy clearing their fields, which are often interspersed with rattan. The field production activities are facilitated by WARSI. Most of the men, teenagers and some children start working at dawn and do not finish until early evening. During this time, their interest in education rapidly declines. They regularly used to come to observe us in the earlier months, but now school is not as crowded. I ask them why and they respond, "It's catch-up time". That means they need to work overtime to collect as much rattan as possible to get ready for the buyers' arrival (who incidentally happen to be WARSI staff).

The students here are quite perplexing. One or two are evidently very bright, but the majority of them are not enthusiastic. It is almost as if school is a duty as opposed to an opportunity. Out of all the children, Beseling is the most interesting. His participation in *sokola* is conditional. He came up with the conditions and I had no choice but to accept them. First, he comes to *sokola* for only one hour. This arrangement is similar to the one he had with Yusak. He said that in the past they only studied at *sokola* for an hour and the rest of the school day was spent chatting and strolling around the jungle. Then, he wanted my assurance that he will be able to master the material being taught within one month. As time went on, Beseling himself realized that this proposal was unrealistic.

"It's impossible, *Ibu*! I'm really slow, aren't I?" He quit school two days before the end of the month.

In Orang Rimba language, *selese sokola* or 'finish school' is to drop out. *Ya*, just like Beseling did. In this case *selese* means to stop one's schooling before the whole process of learning is complete. *Putus sokola* or quit school, on the other hand, contrary to what we understand in Indonesian or in English, means finishing or completing school. Using local terminology, Gentar *putus sokola* while Beseling *selese sokola*. Surprisingly, our eccentric student says he quit school too. He continues to practice his own way of studying by trying to imitate my cursive handwriting. While he has made an excellent effort at copying perfectly, he does not know how to read what he has written.

August 20, 2000
Three munchkins

By nature, Orang Rimba do not take guidance or advice well. It is better that I don't try to coax them to be more diligent. Over the last few *sokola* days, the ones who left school, along with the 'lazy bums', look at Mulung and Pengusay with envy because of their progress in *sokola*. I think this is quite positive.

This morning, at around six-thirty, something unexpected happens. Three young children, between seven and nine years old, take the initiative to come to my hut carrying books and writing materials. They demand to start school immediately. As it turns out, they make this their routine, just the four of us. Wow, so demanding! I can't pretend to be asleep either. They like to peek under my eyelids to see if I am awake. The little munchkins!

They take a nap at noon, and then continue to study until evening. At about eight-thirty in the evening, they excuse themselves and go to sleep. Sometimes, I fall asleep at noon with the kids. We wake up when hunger strikes, or when someone says "The Dutch are here!" This exclamation is used in emergency situations, as apparently the appearance of the Dutch during colonization was considered an emergency.

Hmm, this afternoon nap routine is pretty nice.

August 21, 2000
Rimba men and women

Today, the *rombong* moves three hundred meters away from its previous location. We have to move too because the former site is being prepared as a birthing site or *tana peranaon*. Several pregnant women, very close to giving birth, come to chat there in the afternoon.

I join the women to chat while the children take their afternoon bath in the river to prepare themselves for evening classes. As with women everywhere, they like to discuss men, and men are not allowed to join in. They recount this and that, guy A or B, even discuss sexual matters, after which they all break into peals of laughter.

They are fond of making fun of me, calling me an old maid, or a butch girl for traveling alone. I bet they would get a tummy ache if they were not able to make fun of me for just one day. Normally, I return home before dark, walking to my hut, collecting dry twigs along the way to light a fire. The women's happy chatter and laughter slowly fade into the distance, and then complete silence envelops me. Hmm, this life is truly peaceful.

How much more fortunate it is to be a Rimba woman than a Rimba man. Just look at the men. They sweat and work until their muscles pop out. They slog it out for their women and children, transporting rattan from deep within the rainforest. And they arrive home to be greeted by their wives saying, "Is that all?" He he he . . . despite their wives' provocative remarks, Rimba men tend not to lose their tempers. At most, they grumble.

From childhood, Rimba men are conditioned to practice self-restraint in anger, appetite, material greed and sexual urges as well. On the other side of the spectrum, the women are left at liberty. Their attitude is that men are responsible for the well being of the family, including women and children. The men are expected to repress their ego. Greedy men are selfish. A lazy man is a bad catch for a woman and is also an unattractive son-in-law.

Fussy, demanding and materialistic traits in women are considered virtues. Constantly demanding that the husband hunts and plants crops ensures sufficient household supplies. It guarantees that children will be well fed and secure. An easygoing woman causes a husband to be slothful. It is no wonder then, that the sound of angry female chatter, brassy and loud, is the norm. The men's voices, timid, almost inaudible, mostly say only, "*Au . . . au . . .*" (All right, all right . . .) Or they simply ignore the verbal onslaught, as if it were their routine mode of conversing. Very rarely do the men return the aggression. In fact, I have never encountered this.

I feel assured and calm in this seemingly matriarchal community. Even the cruelest Rimba man is highly unlikely to molest or rape a woman. I actually worry that if there were a case of rape, a Rimba female would likely be the rapist!

For the Orang Rimba "to be a man" implies outstanding moral qualities, bordering on nobility. Often times we hear, "*Awok jenton!*" (We are men!) It is an expression uttered among men to remind themselves of their proud standing as men. The men are responsible for protecting Rimba women and children from attacks from the outside world, wild beasts and famine. In any dispute pitting a man against a woman, the woman almost always wins. Similarly, if the woman is fined, the man is fined equally.

One of their traditional rhymes illustrates Rimba gender relationships well:

Duriyon titik podo mentimun,
Mentimun hancur
Mentimun begolek podo duriyon,
Mentimun jugo nang hancur.

When a durian falls on a cucumber,
The cucumber will be crushed.
When the cucumber leans against the durian,
It will still be crushed!

The durian here represents the woman, and the cucumber is the man. Regardless of who falls on or touches whom, the cucumber gets hurt or destroyed by the durian's sharp spikes. It does not matter where the mistake resides, the man always pays the price. It is only a question of how much.

One exception perhaps is in the event a woman changes her mind about a marriage, as that involves returning her dowry.

August 22, 2000
New method of reading

I discover a new method of teaching spelling in the jungle. The sound *ng* as an ending remains the same regardless of which letters precede it. For example BANG, BING, BUNG, BENG, BONG, YANG, YING etc. This pattern is a useful spelling device giving students confidence with simple spelling tasks. Linca's group expands on this idea by using a three-in-one technique encouraging the students to pronounce words without sounding out individual letters. In the three-in-one technique, the students read three letters in one go, or one syllable that is comprised of three "characters". The "ng" is considered one character. Examples they use include: TAS (bag), DAN (and) and YANG (which).

I begin to notice that the students are reluctant to write creatively and are unwilling to use their own initiative when spelling new words. In spelling, their accuracy rate tends to be around forty percent. So far, I have created sixteen different levels to achieve this target My aim is to attain reading and writing skills at the fifteenth level. In math, they are now familiar with numbers up to ten and can carry out simple addition with numbers up to twenty. Addition and subtraction skills will not be consolidated until the month's end. Basically, I want their math and reading standards to reach a second grade level.

Gentar, the teacher trainee

Gentar's teaching internship at Air Hitam yields surprisingly positive results. He is able to cover eighty percent of the prepared teaching material in six days without my presence. I see the children are also able to apply what they have learned from Gentar.

Throughout my time in the field, Gentar seems overwhelmed when he does everything himself. He is very focused on reaching the *sokola* teaching targets that I proposed. Now and then, he becomes too absorbed and drives his students too hard toward the target, boring them. The month before when Linca was around, they took turns covering each other's duties. Now that Gentar is alone, there is less lesson variation.

Anticipating this, I equip myself with a soccer ball to play with the children. As it happens, they like the game and become engrossed in it. If anyone watches us play, they will not guess that we are playing soccer. The kids jostle around the ball and, when they kick it, the ball usually ends up ten meters off the field. We spend more time collecting the ball than playing with it. The ball does not last very long. Well, what can be expected from a cheap, plastic ball? Yet, the children never run out of ideas. The damaged ball is filled with masses of paper and leaves, then fastened by a tangle of roots, and off they go to play again.

Overall, Gentar deals with any speed bumps that come his way. He pushes on with his work despite being ill with a fever and cough for three days. Likewise, he becomes quite close to his loyal students. And he gets on well with the men in this group. They begin to regard him as one of their relatives. After a while *Tengganai* Meratai for example calls him 'grandchild' (and continues to do so to this day.)

I hope Gentar becomes an instructor of future teacher trainees. For me, he is the male version of Kartini, the Indonesian pioneer in educating girls; Gentar is a pioneer in the field of Orang Rimba education. He may lack some leadership qualities; he tends to dither about making decisions and is too cautious, afraid of making mistakes. Linca's initiative and creativity, though impulsive at times, balance this out. To me, they are perfectly complementary. Lately, Gentar has been saying he misses Linca and that he prefers to work in a team rather than alone. He thinks that he will ask Linca to come and work with him next month.

August 24, 2000
Hunting for teaching recruits

While teaching at Air Hitam, I keep a vigilant watch for potential future teacher trainees. I think that maybe Mulung is a candidate. He is the fifth child in a family of nine. This is to my advantage. Usually it is more complicated with the first-born because of their responsibility for younger family members and to their parents to help hunt for food in the jungle. Although Mulung has a small build, he is the most productive worker at bringing money home. Apart from that, he is smart, always smiling and kind-hearted. He has his own vision of the future and the kind of life he would like to lead when he grows up.

In this regard, he is similar to Gentar. He likes the self-sufficiency of the Orang Rimba lifestyle but is open-minded enough to adopt appropriate elements of the *Orang Terang's* life. The only stumbling block is that he is not very approachable. He is reserved, quiet and cautious. Having said that, he is also physically active and energetic. He is here, there and everywhere non-stop. He works and studies hard.

Another candidate is Pengusay, the late Yusak's former student. He has the same vision as Linca, who wants to be like the *Orang Terang*. And, he has the same reserved personality as Mulung.

I am not sure. How is one supposed to teach if one is too shy to speak? Rumor has it that Pengusay, who was engaged to Ngali, the young daughter of *Bepak* Terenong, was just rejected by her. He devoted the last three years of his life to her family in *semendo* as required by the customary law and tradition of the Orang Rimba during engagement. Unbelievable! The sacrifices these Rimba men make for love seem so sweet.

Mulung and Pengusay buy their own interesting writing materials. They also buy relatively modern school bags at the SP 1 market. The school has caught the attention of the SP I market vendors. They realize these children are beginning to purchase items they have never touched before. The people at market *Pasar* SP B Tanagaro make the same observation. I talk to the market and village people and I gather their reactions are mixed. Some are positive while others remain skeptical.

My colleague at WARSI shared a strange anecdote about what he discovered at the Orang Rimba school (named by the government: *Suku Anak Dalam* or school for the isolated people) at Pematang Kabau, which was built by the government. My colleague met with the schoolteacher who proudly praised one of his pupils for successfully attaining a sixth grade level in six years. However, having tested him, my colleague assessed the student's speed and accuracy in reading and writing as not much better than Linca's level after just five months of studying. *Astaga!* What has he been doing for the last six years? I met a child studying in grade two at the primary school, a village child, who was practically illiterate. He could only write his name. And that too was only through memorization.

August 25, 2000
"Treats for the circus performer"

I leave Air Hitam. Gentar joins me as far as Bangko. He wants to purchase some things like clothing, food for the family, and rifle ammunition for his stepfather. He does not buy even one item for himself. Apparently, he creates a positive impression at one of the big shops in Bangko. Talking to him, they are impressed by his cleverness and straight-forwardness. A vendor treats him to free food and drink, moved by his ability to read certain words. Others generously present him with this and that or else simply give him discounts.

Even though I am happy that some people are appreciative of Gentar, I feel that others are not so genuine. It is as if these people are testing to see how high a circus animal can jump using food as a lure. They are not sincere in accepting Gentar as an equal member of the human race. Oh, I hope this is just my imagination . . .

The continuation of Sokola

The moment after I am picked up at the jungle's edge by the office car, issues and thoughts flood my head. My brain cannot stop thinking even though my body is incredibly tired. I am sleep-deprived from working overtime to create lesson plans for the children. Not to mention my growling stomach, I long for a juicy piece of fried chicken with *sambal*, but I realize that I still have a lot of work to do.

I think about spending regular time with the Orang Rimba, about the continuation of *sokola*. There is also the need for follow-up on the matter of employing new teacher recruits. I wonder how to organize things if Mulung becomes involved. I think that Mulung has excellent potential as a teacher trainee. He personifies the combined characters of Gentar and Linca. There is another advantage. He is very young and thus can teach for longer than Gentar, who may have to stop in two or three years to get married.

I also try to figure out how to increase Gentar's commitment. What kind of arrangement will work? I have no experience in personnel matters but I am aware that the *sokola* can easily lose people like Gentar. The pressing educational needs of the Orang Rimba make a decision even more urgent.

Aah!! My mind is spinning . . . How can I apply these methods to other groups? How should Sokola Rimba be organized? What is its future? Just thinking about all this is exhausting and nerve-racking, yet exciting.

At the office, a colleague in charge of the Orang Rimba at Terap River asks if I will try to approach a neighboring group. Apparently, this group has been under intense pressure from the outside world. Hmm . . . if visits to the Orang Rimba staying in the Terap River area go smoothly, I could combine the teaching team from Bernai and Air Hitam to work in Terap. Eventually a team could be formed comprising instructors from each location or *rombong* rotating around Bukit Dua Belas. Wow . . . This is getting me excited! Fingers crossed . . .

August 29, 2000
Workshop at WARSI

I am a little disappointed that WARSI does not adopt my idea of employing Gentar and Linca to staff my Education Section. I think this would have proven both to the teacher trainees and to WARSI that this is a serious working relationship. It seems WARSI thinks otherwise. Several reasons are given such as avoiding jealousy among the students and not having enough funds for the proposal. The more pertinent reason is that WARSI is not ready to have outside people in its workshops. If there were instances where discussions involved negative talk about the Orang Rimba, it would be inappropriate to have Gentar or Linca there.

Now what? How do I sustain the *sokola* and continue the practice that each Orang Rimba group should teach its own people? Am I supposed to teach them all on my own as a WARSI staff member, covering all of this vast Rimba territory? For how long? So far, WARSI does not seem to have any contingency plan either. Meanwhile, I have to stay committed as the only education facilitator. Naturally, as a WARSI employee, I should abide by the institution's decisions. It's true, but . . .

Memories from the Jungle

Rimba Paparazzi

The children made stone sculptures of cameras and cell phones mimicking outsiders. Penangguk is taking pictures with his "camera".

Off-Road Driving

A car gets stuck deep in the jungle.

Butet Riding a Motorbike

Playing Tarzan

Dodi, a teacher at the Jungle School once said, "When I was a kid, I played Tarzan, pretending my city neighborhood was a jungle. As an adult, I play with real Tarzans in the real jungle!"

Say Cheese!

Siyomban, the hunter, with his wild boar

Slingshot Warriors

Recess at Sokola Rimba—Mud Sliding!

Traditional Medicine

Mijak spreads an herbal rub on the chest to treat pain caused by heavy coughing.

Butet with Orang Rimba Women

Most Orang Rimba rombong forbid smoking for women until they reach menopause, so it is unusual to see a young woman with a cigarette. Even commercially made cigarettes are unusual as the Orang Rimba roll their own tobacco. This cigarette was a gift from a visitor. Recently, smokers have begun to barter rattan for cigarettes—it's more efficient than harvesting, drying, and chopping tobacco.

Butet Teaches School by the River

School Lunch Program—Collecting Snails

I was a very poor trapper and never managed to catch any game in my traps. Lucky for me, I enjoy eating river snails.

Morning Routine at the Schoolhouse

Night School

Sometimes we held classes in the evening. Here we are in Kedundung Jehat in 2004.

New Girl in Class

Having a girl in class makes the boys and me nervous—what if the adults object and stop the class. I am secretly excited to think that perhaps all the girls might come to school one day.

Butet with Her Students

Self-appointed Orang Rimba "School Supervisor"

A supervisor can inspect your school, even without 24 hours notice, in the jungle. The supervisor/mom may visit to make sure you are teaching the children properly and are sensitive to their culture or simply to have a free lunch. Every once in a while, the supervisor arrived with a big chunk of boar meat to share.

Self-Portrait by Menosur

School with Solar Panels

The motorbike in the foreground and the solar panels both reached this area after 2006.

Schoolhouse, 2008

The school at Sako Napu that was funded by a major sponsor and is the best school building to date.

Indit with Jungle Bodyguards

In the jungle, there are always small bodyguards ready to escort us. Small children always accompany us as we travel, protecting us from snakes, bears and boars and making sure we don't get lost!

Community-based Advocacy for the National Park

Jungle Guardian

To me, this is a monumental photo—an Orang Rimba boy questioning this marker that was placed in the jungle by the government. The Orang Rimba inhabited this jungle long before the State began determining boundaries within it. These boundary markers represent a change to the Orang Rimba's habitat, livelihood and way of life.

Part 2

Looking Back

Chapter 1

Looking Forward, Looking Back

June 2003

My life with the Orang Rimba lasted longer than I had imagined. Without realizing it, I have spent four years in the rainforest. The Orang Rimba education program, which I had doubted would succeed, continued smoothly, and to some extent even grew and developed.

I have had countless difficult and confusing times with the Orang Rimba. I remember how they rejected me at first, but now they demand my presence everywhere. My proposal to draw teacher trainees from within the Orang Rimba community is progressing. We were nurturing fourteen young Rimba trainees. However, seven trainees got married and had to leave the program to look after their families. The remaining seven continue to work as a team, carrying out the program and believing in its importance.

How many students have there been? I directly taught around a hundred children. Under my co-ordination and tutorship of three generations of teachers, we have taught around three hundred children.

I did some quick calculations. According to a WARSI survey, there are roughly 1,250 Orang Rimba. If a family consists of six members, then there are over 200 families. One household on average has four children, making a total of more than 800 children. Assuming an equal division between genders, there would be about 400 boys. Most of our students are male. We have only six female students. So, nearly 75% of male children have participated in the education program. This result is based on WARSI's data.

However, by my rough calculation, with some help from the Rimba children, there are more likely 3,500 Orang Rimba. Based on this estimate and my previous assumptions, only about 25% of the boys are literate.

What were the immediate positive outcomes of the program? How did the Rimba children benefit from schooling? They can now count and multiply correctly; this gives them a level of competence in dealing with most of their market and employment transactions. For example, they can read the numbers shown on the scales at the market and understand whether the needle points to five hundred grams or ten kilograms.

Other benefits come with being able to read. The Orang Rimba *rombong* at Makekal Hulu are involved in a dispute with villagers who manage a plantation in the rainforest. Each side feels they are right. The Orang Rimba claim that the village people have breached an agreement reached several years ago about the location of boundaries between point x and y. The villagers insist that they have not violated the agreement. The Orang Rimba's claim is based on memory because they were unable to read the agreement. Consequently, the village people are suspicious because the Orang Rimba made claims that differ from the written record of the agreement.

There is another possible scenario. The village people may have based their understanding of the boundary on what they read in the agreement. However, the Orang Rimba recollection of this boundary was possibly accurate, but their location was not verified when the agreement was written down. After much dispute, it is agreed that both sides will make a new accord.

When it is time to sign this new agreement with a thumbprint, one of my students interrupts. He says to their elders, "Stop, let us read it aloud first. You can put your thumbprint on the agreement after you have listened to it." My student, Penyuruk, slowly reads the new terms.

Everyone listens carefully to each word that he recites. The elders start whispering, and the *temenggung* listens attentively, full of amazement. *Mangku* Ngidin, Penyuruk's stepfather, proudly says to the villager sitting near him, "That is my son! He has been going to school in this Rimba." Some of the villagers are in awe, but others have sullen faces. I stand in a corner following the proceeding.

Once it was read, everybody enthusiastically approves the agreement. Penyuruk looks around for me to ask for my approval. I smile and give him a thumbs-up. His smile widens, like a ten-year-old who has been complimented by his parents. What a great feeling! I am so proud of him.

This is also an example of how dangerous it is for the Orang Rimba to remain illiterate. Yet, it is not an easy journey. I think back to the time

I first came to *Mangku* Ngidin's *rombong*. He rejected me and sent me away with a threat saying he would smash my head in. Now, after this event, he treats me like his adopted daughter.

While I am proud of my students' accomplishments, I have mixed emotions. Should the Orang Rimba face anything more complex than this agreement, I am confident my students can handle it! However, I still don't feel at ease. There is still a pebble in my shoe and it is bothering me.

I am especially bothered by the children's innocent yet fundamental questions. "*Ibu guru*, why is the rainforest still disappearing? I thought if we went to school, there would be no need for logging or palm oil plantations or transmigration projects. I thought education would help us to overcome all these problems." I see a parallel to my brother questioning my mother, "Ma, why is there murder and robbery? I thought if people believed in God and practiced their religion, they would not do these bad things."

Along with these occasional prodding questions from the children, the attitude of some of my colleagues toward education also disturbs me. During my second year with the Orang Rimba, I wanted to resign from WARSI to continue my studies. My plan was not received positively. "Why don't you wait until you have 100 students?"

The following year when I had around 180 students, they procrastinated again. "Why don't you wait until you have 200 students?" This approach, emphasizing quantity over quality, focuses on increasing literacy figures rather than on the depth and range of literacy targets.

I acknowledge that my colleagues were struggling with their own priorities relating to rainforest conservation. Orang Rimba education simply complemented the conservation work. Maybe they thought, "Let the Orang Rimba experience education and improve their literacy so they can help us with conservation. Later, if they are still interested, they can pursue their education further themselves."

If their aim was solely to increase the number of students, it made me feel like I was following the same pattern as with missionaries: increase the number of students, baptize them with reading and writing, then potentially abandon them. I thought about how missionaries, like NGOs, love statistics, although their aim is to spread religion. They count the "fruit of the harvest" annually. For example, the Christian missionaries are quite happy when there is an increase in the number of Papuans or Dayaks converted to Christianity. The same is the case for Islamic missionaries; they are pleased when there is an increase in the number of *kafir Kubu* (primitive infidels) in Bukit Dua Belas who convert to Islam.

In reality, many of the converts do not actually practice their beliefs whole-heartedly. They often just use their allocation of perishable food items, or accept housing or land, which can then be resold to the villagers for money.

I want my students to be able to take on the challenge of defending their rights. The rights of the Orang Rimba are not just about their habitat, the issue that has been hotly pursued during my entire time in the jungle. There are other aspects to this struggle, including their right to determine their way of life.

The issues are huge, our response miniscule. One tiny drop of education in the form of basic literacy is not sufficient to cope with such fundamental changes and challenges. Is the ability to read and write really such a panacea? Or am I just too naïve?

There is so much more to know. A *bepak* sneers at his child because he cannot answer questions like:

"Where is Aceh?"

"Why does the river become more shallow every year?"

Or (sighing), "Why aren't you able to speak enough Indonesian to chat with *Orang Luar* (the outsiders) about problems and their solutions?"

"Why can't you write a complaint letter about illegal logging in the rainforest? You don't even know where to send it, do you?"

"Why do prices go up? People say the government reduced their subsidy because of too much overseas debt. What is a subsidy? What is overseas debt? Why not just print more money to pay the debt?"

I often find that the Orang Rimba are at a loss when they are in the "other world". They often ask questions like: "How can airplanes fly?" or "How can this radio box make sound?" They struggle with the terminology of this "other world". They ask "Why are the houses so big? Why do some cars live in houses (garages)? Why are houses built for cars, while some people live on the street (as homeless people or beggars) without a roof over their heads?" Once, when some of my students and I visited Jakarta, a student asked, "Why do cars sleep inside at night while those people sleep in cardboard boxes under the bridge?"

While driving on the highway in Jakarta, "Normally, there is a river under a bridge, but here there is a road with cars. Why do you have to have so many roads?"

When they saw fountains in the city they were perplexed, *"Ibu,* look at that, the water goes from the ground upwards. Normally, water flows down, that is the nature of water, isn't that what you told us?"

I know from my experience with Orang Rimba children that they are astute enough to comprehend the outside world. Teachers can use various devices to explain the unfamiliar, comparing it to the Orang Rimba world and their cultural context. The use of age-appropriate concepts and language is also helpful. Besides, the children are quite capable of finding the answers to all their questions without their teachers. This is clear whenever I hear my students responding to each other's questions.

Can these simple, yet fundamental, questions be answered with *only* reading and writing skills? This position ignores the well-recognized importance of a broad and tailored education. And I only give examples of a few of their questions. They have many other, more probing questions like:

"Why are there bad people and good people?" This question was in response to a newspaper article dealing with rape, stealing and murder. These crimes are unheard of in Orang Rimba communities.

"Why was I born an Orang Rimba?" This question was asked by one of my pupils in 2001. Many Orang Rimba felt the pressure of prejudice in the outside world. These feelings arose during negotiations with people from the outside world who had no understanding of or respect for the Rimba or their situation.

"Can I be a doctor like *Ibu* Ati?" In the early days of SOKOLA, students assumed that reading and writing skills alone would be enough to become a doctor.

"Why do women in the outside world go out by themselves or with men other than their husbands?" In Orang Rimba communities, gender roles and relations are strictly controlled.

"Why do people in the outside world have more than one set of clothes? Sometimes even a closet full of clothes . . ."

And, one of my favorites, "Those people sitting in offices for hours, what do they do?"

All these questions bother me. I want to create a broader education curriculum that enables the Orang Rimba to engage successfully with the outside world. And, I know that WARSI has only a limited capacity to deliver educational programs that go beyond basic literacy. Their focus is primarily on rainforest conservation, which is extremely frustrating to me as an educator. WARSI's position makes me think of my own stance. What is the best approach for the Orang Rimba? Is my approach just as flawed?

The Orang Rimba and the tide of change

In July 2002, a friend from Norway visited the Rimba. When he left, my students wanted to send him a letter. At the WARSI office, I typed their letter as an email. One hour later, we received a reply. The children looked around when I told them that my friend had replied to their letter.

"Where is he? How did he deliver his letter?"

I printed the reply using a printer in another room. The children were flummoxed to see that the letter was now on paper. They asked me to re-print it so that they could go stand in front of the printer and see how it worked.

"Oh, I understand," they said proudly pointing to the printer's cable "The letters come through here! But how do the letters run so fast?"

They were so excited; we got carried away writing and answering letters until late in the evening. I could feel the glares of disapproval from my office colleagues. My students and I returned to the rainforest the following morning.

At the next monthly meeting, my colleagues accused me of making a serious mistake by introducing the Orang Rimba children to the rudiments of communications technology. They said that it wasn't good for the children. To be more precise, emails and computers do not fit WARSI's "idea of conservation".

WARSI believes that the Orang Rimba should not be exposed to the outside world, which will leave them less oriented towards the conservation of the forest.

"Why can't they use email here? Email can be an excellent medium for their intellectual development," I asked. My question was refuted by a lengthy, meandering answer, in which some of my WARSI colleagues reasoned that the Orang Rimba would face culture shock. I did not understand this reasoning, but it's pretty difficult for me to understand WARSI at the best of times anyway.

I received a similar response when I was posted to teach in the southeastern part of Bukit Dua Belas area. Linca asked me to show him how to drive a motorcycle. I was staying overnight on the periphery of the rainforest in a village with a soccer field. By coincidence, my co-worker had the office motorcycle with him. So, the situation was perfect for Linca. I taught him about the brakes, the throttle and how to change gears. Suddenly, I was reprimanded by my colleague. "Why are you teaching him to ride?" he asked.

I was puzzled as to why I was not allowed to teach him. It was quite rational. Just imagine if he could use a motorcycle to transport rubber sap from the edge of the rainforest to the village, it would only take thirty minutes. On foot, it takes seven hours, twelve hours including the return trip. The time and energy wasted could be used to do other things.

Another time, a WARSI co-worker returned from the Makekal Hulu River shocked to find children wearing shorts and not loincloths. He was furious and accused me of influencing this change. This became such a big concern that we discussed it in the next workshop. They decided not to send me to that *rombong* again, to stop my "bad" influence. So, in early 2003 I was transferred to Bukit Tiga Puluh National Park, between Jambi and Riau province.

I was stunned. The Orang Rimba should be able to choose to wear shorts or buy a motorcycle. Do we have the moral authority to say they have violated their own customs? An American anthropologist, doing research on the Rimba, and Dodi, an anthropologist friend of mine for the last fifteen years, both assured me that I was not at fault.

The Rimba people have the right to change and this change will come whether or not I am in this jungle. The Orang Rimba can decide which aspects of this change they wish to embrace. It is quite possible that they are not yet fully aware of the consequences of their choices. However, that is not a reason for us to prohibit them from making these choices.

A person's identity is a complex matter. This is even more true for Orang Rimba facing the tide of change. We cannot judge the Orang Rimba's shifting identity on the basis of their change of clothing. Wearing or not wearing a loincloth does not make them more or less Orang Rimba. We become anxious, perhaps paranoid; as if the presence of modern goods is proof that the Orang Rimba we know no longer exist.

Let's look at some other propositions. If the Orang Rimba change will their efforts to conserve the rainforests be undermined? Does it also follow that eventually they will not need the rainforest anymore?

The Orang Rimba's habitat and the world's rainforests are slowly shrinking. I have not heard of a rainforest that is expanding with increasing biodiversity. Most stories we hear are about the worsening conditions, the increasing rate of loss, and the destruction of rainforests.

The level of rainforest destruction in Indonesia has nearly reached that of Brazil. How can this be possible? Just imagine the size of 3.8 million hectares being destroyed per year. Who is the main perpetrator of this destruction?

Bukit Dua Belas, the Orang Rimba's habitat, is the tiniest National Park in Indonesia. It is regarded as a landmark, symbolizing a triumphant conclusion to an enduring struggle. Jambi now has five National Parks, an improvement from three (Berbak National Park, Kerinci Seblat National Park, Bukit Tiga Puluh National Park), and bringing Jambi's National Park area to several million hectares. What is involved in the expansion of a National Park? If we simply need to draw lines around existing rainforests, then marker posts can be put up around the whole of Jambi to declare the entire province one huge National Park!

Park area statistics can be deceptive. There are no measurements to show how many trees with trunks of more than a meter in diameter are still standing. Similarly, decreases in the water table are not monitored annually and neither are other changes like the disappearance of traditional medicinal plants, or the extinction of elephants and great hornbills or the vanishing populations of Sumatran tigers. At Bukit Dua Belas, there has been absolutely no change in management or protection even though it is now a National Park whose area has doubled in size. In addition, like other National Parks in Indonesia, this rainforest is full of large barren patches.

As the condition of the Orang Rimba habitat further declines, the *Orang Terang* offer an alternative way of life outside the rainforest with a new religion and money from the palm oil plantations. There is so much to think about and figure out. How is palm oil used? Is it hard to grow the palms? What's in it for me? What is Islam? What does it offer? What am I supposed to do every day?

Yet, how can anyone make a choice if they don't really understand the options, if they don't have the facts and figures to make comparisons and decide which alternative is best?

I feel a duty to explain every choice to the Orang Rimba objectively, without an agenda. I am not an agent with a particular ideology or a pawn with a vested interest. My only agenda is the independence of the Orang Rimba, their fulfillment, and the pursuit of their definition of happiness.

This takes me back to my original hypothetical question: Would a healthy and well-cared-for rainforest solve the Orang Rimba's problems? Is the dilemma of the Orang Rimba that simple? Can the larger question of the Orang Rimba's livelihood be reduced to simply helping them to avoid being cheated in trade and land negotiations?

The Orang Rimba are often presented as a people who live a constrained life, deserving pity because of the inevitable degradation they will suffer from the pressures of the outside world. This view dominates the media. It is rare to see images of the Orang Rimba as optimistic, cheerful, empowered or capable. The media seem to ignore all of this. This pessimistic image has even caused the Orang Rimba to pity themselves. It is as if the Orang Rimba have been trained to wallow in their perceived pessimism.

Contrary to our intentions, outsiders also reinforce feelings of powerlessness sometimes simply by offering to help. It makes complete sense if the Orang Rimba give in to this image of themselves and begin to hope for aid from outsiders rather than make an effort or through their own initiative.

This was clearly apparent when WARSI asked me to accompany some journalists into the rainforest. Our task was to support the journalists and "ensure their success" by providing suitable material to highlight the threats to the Orang Rimba habitat. This expedition was financed by WARSI. The brief included the need to show how the Orang Rimba were skilled at living in the rainforest. A number of print journalists from Jambi were invited, as well as the local branch of a Jakarta television station. WARSI provided three staff: Oceu and me from the education section, and Dodi, an anthropologist.

So here we are waiting in the jungle for the contingent of journalists. There are fourteen journalists covering this event. *Aduh*, even one is a headache, but fourteen! This situation irritates me. I have already been asked too many times to accompany journalists writing stories about the Orang Rimba. The main purpose of this media event is to inform the general public that Orang Rimba children are going to school. The fact that the school is in the middle of the jungle is interesting, indeed unique.

I start to become annoyed with answering questions to help set the scene for these journalists. On one hand it is an opportunity to voice Orang Rimba concerns about losing their way of life; on the other, I feel like a monkey in a street performance, applauded by the audience after each show.

The journalists, accompanied by one of the WARSI communications staff, arrive at one-thirty in the morning and plan to leave at ten the same morning. Mind you, that includes sleeping time. What can they cover in just a few hours? Can this even be called an expedition?

They wake me up. The television journalist asks me to prepare a night class right away for filming. I feel pressured to meet their request and am told repeatedly that everything had been discussed and agreed upon at the office. Dodi, Oceu and I protest. We look at the Rimba children, still sleeping.

Ah, it is happening again. People at the office often discuss my Orang Rimba work without me. They don't feel the need to talk to me, much less to ask my opinion. Just look at this. The set-up really irritates me. The plan is to get a few children to cross the river and fetch more children, then come to my hut to study. All the students have to change into their loincloths. We also have to create artificial conversations. We are stunned. Finally, I oblige and do it unhappily. I have to force the children to co-operate. They are not happy and Peniti Benang even cries. "*Ibu guru*, I don't want to, I am very sleepy. It's night time, it is too cold to go into the river," he says.

I cajole, I half-order him. Ah . . . I get so stressed even thinking about this incident.

"Come on, Benang, do it now so we can go back to sleep again later."

"But, why not tomorrow? It is late already, and I don't want to wear a loincloth." This is true, not all Rimba children wear loincloths.

Finally, the children give in. I know this pleases the journalists, but I feel that I have manipulated the children. I feel like I have committed a sin against them.

We proceed with this "Study in the Night" soap opera. Dodi and Oceu look at me with pity. Then, Dodi and Oceu join in, teaching art and general science. I laugh at them, or more correctly, we laugh at this ridiculous situation we find ourselves in. I remember the slogan "Education ensures liberty." In this case, even the teachers are enslaved! He he he . . .

We go to bed at dawn, around four o'clock in the morning. At eight o'clock we start "the show" again. They film the Orang Rimba's daily activities: climbing the honey tree, mixing traditional medicines, preserving the sacred trees and so on. They focus on any aspect of their daily lives that supports the notion that the Orang Rimba need their rainforest and they know how to take care of it.

I am sullen and my mind is elsewhere. Still, I try to occupy the children with studying or chores. We collect firewood and cook for the journalists.

While we are cooking, one of the journalists walks over to the river. Suddenly, he cries out. He thinks he has stumbled over some kind of root. I stare at the children, each of them fully aware of what has happened. One of them lowers his head; it must have been his trap. The journalist's foot is caught in a trap set by one of the students. Sometimes, this is how they teach a lesson to outsiders they don't like. The children surround me, as if ready to take orders. Their have a cheeky smirk on their faces.

Their faces are even gloomier when the journalists bombard them with questions.

"How old are you?" (Um, the Orang Rimba have no concept of age.)

"What do your parents do?" (All Orang Rimba do the same thing—hunting and planting, if that qualifies as work by the journalists.)

"What is your dream, your goal?" (The Orang Rimba ask back, "What is a dream? Why have a goal?")

"What grade are you in?" (The Orang Rimba children are confused. The journalists cannot fathom a school without grades).

"When do you want to leave the jungle?" (The Orang Rimba are just plain confused.)

"Don't you want to live in the city?" (The Orang Rimba are even more confused and agitated.)

"Will you convert to Islam or Christianity?" (Now the Orang Rimba are really offended and say, "We have our own religion!")

True, it is not totally the journalists' fault, but their questions annoy the children. This story is a classic example of a case where both sides have little knowledge of the other. The journalists who come armed with a city person's perspective obviously have some difficulty understanding the world from the Orang Rimba perspective, especially understanding their lifestyle. It's not surprising that their perception of the Orang Rimba is always a pessimistic one. They are on the wrong track from the very start!

In truth, I do appreciate the journalists' efforts. They are mounting a campaign directed at the preservation of the rainforest and trying to help the Orang Rimba. They can do this by providing a more detailed picture of their lives. They can also organize meetings with influential people who can support the protection of the Bukit Dua Belas Park. Nevertheless, at times, these events do resemble cheap melodramas.

There are other frustrations. I often get annoyed when the outside world holds meetings with the Orang Rimba. The organizers say that the Orang Rimba need to be "facilitated" through the conversation. Interactions are normally conducted by the *Orang Luar* in Indonesian, which is translated for the Orang Rimba, and then the Orang Rimba's response is translated back into Indonesian. Consequently, the facilitator often ends up becoming a translator. I think this method of communication gives the impression that the Orang Rimba are somehow powerless. Worse yet, in some meetings, the translator just speaks on behalf of the Orang Rimba, "Blah, blah, blah." When he is done, he turns to the Orang Rimba representative and says, "Isn't that right, *Bepak*?"

The Orang Rimba community must represent themselves, voice their own needs and have their own point of view. Self-representation avoids an over-reliance on intermediaries to communicate with the outside world. In their own words, the Rimba can articulate in greater detail and with force their own views and identity, their own rights and needs.

My dream is to have one of my students speak up with humility and confidence in a forum. Building confidence is important. Whenever possible I include in my lessons various topics which will nurture their self-respect and pride. Hopefully, this addresses the erosive influences of the outside world, like the use of the derogatory term *"Kubu"*, which has been used for years as a substitute word for Orang Rimba.

As I see it, as soon as the Orang Rimba have a clear perspective about where they stand and their predicament, they will be able to think independently. I am confident that they will find a way out, as the Orang Rimba always do. Another wish is for the Orang Rimba, when faced with outside pressures, to take a stand and decide freely for themselves what to do.

Having said this, I remember one idea proposed by the Rimba children. In 2002, the children came to Dodi and me and said that they wanted to form a battalion of rainforest wardens. They thought that, with this organization, they could prevent theft from the rainforest. They wanted to protect the jungle. We discussed this project energetically. *Ya*, they would be perfect wardens as they would be "disguised" as ordinary Orang Rimba. The thieves would not suspect anything as the Orang Rimba were considered ignorant. They would not know that now the Orang Rimba could take notes.

The Rimba could write down the thieves' names and other details such as where, how many people are involved, what kind of wood is being stolen and where it is being sold. The children asked for some material support such as a camera, a GPS and a satellite phone. *Wah*, we ourselves were never supplied with all this equipment when in the field. They also asked for a supply of provisions because they would not be able to look for food.

They would call themselves *Pasukan Rimba Bungaron Rayo* (the Bungaron Rayo Rainforest Battalion) or Unit PRBR. They collected money for Dodi to have uniforms made for them in Bandung, West Java. Orang Rimba adore uniforms, whatever style, reflecting rank and company. They saw how the uniformed people in the outside world (defense personnel, police, doctors) were treated with respect.

Not long after, Dodi returned from his home in Bandung with green military uniforms. He bought them at Jatayu, the second-hand market in Bandung that sells military uniforms. They were so very proud to have these dark green military outfits, with a badge on the left sleeve depicting a mouse deer, exactly like a Boy Scout badge. On the left side of the chest was the red and white flag of Indonesia.

"Why is there a mouse deer?" the children asked.

"Because mouse deer are smart and cunning and they suit you. Once you've established yourselves, then we can change to a stag. And when you get even better, we'll change to a tiger. If you mess up, we'll change to a leech. If you mess up even more, we'll make the badge a mosquito," Dodi answered.

They all laughed.

On one shirt the flag patch came off, so one of the children sewed it back on, but upside down. I said to him "You've sown it the wrong way. See, it's white and red, not red and white."

"Oh yeah . . ." So, he took off his shirt and put it back on upside down. "It's red and white now."

Dodi and I were thrilled to organize this new group. We were very optimistic about the plan and confident of WARSI's support.

Much to our dismay, the plan was torn apart and rejected. They thought it was a stupid idea. They said it was madness and too dangerous. It could create enemies for WARSI. Wardens were the domain of the Forestry Department, not WARSI. My duty was to provide education, that's it. And Dodi, as an anthropologist, was supposed to distance himself from the Orang Rimba. He was there to observe, not to get involved.

WARSI did not want to take any responsibility for anything associated with this scheme. There were a host of other objections that I cannot now recall. In retrospect, what is a struggle without risks? I was very sad, and the Rimba children were angry. I thought that they somehow felt disappointed in me for not defending the idea more vigorously at the WARSI meeting.

Nevertheless, although the unit was not officially sanctioned, the Rimba had a chance to go around in the rainforest with their own agenda. Even *Temenggung* Mirak accompanied them a couple of times. However, they could not be wardens all the time because they also had to look for food for themselves and their families.

After a month, they said to me, "*Ibu guru,* we should change our name. Not PRBR but Bramatala."

"What is Bramatala?"

"It is the brave heart unit. It stands for BRAni MAti TAkut LApar—ready to die, but afraid to starve!"

Oh, they make me laugh!

At that point in time, I felt empty. I had lost my direction and the children seemed disappointed in me. I felt there was an insinuation in the name "Bramatala". Did I fear losing my job so much that I didn't have the nerve to stand up for what I believed? Honestly, yes, I did fear losing my job. I just loved this position so much, but at the same time I felt so constrained. My mother, too, had become so concerned while listening to my grievances that she suggested I look for another job.

The failure to set up a Rainforest Warden unit was quite a blow for me. At the same time, I was really perplexed. Their initiative to defend the rainforest seemed like genuine progress toward higher self-awareness. They realized that they possessed the right, they had the correct idea, and they wanted to act on it. I was having difficulty thinking clearly. My senior colleagues at WARSI frequently advised me to maintain a distance from the Orang Rimba. But this time, I just could not tolerate it.

It concerns me and makes me angry when the Orang Rimba are pushed around by different interest groups. Whatever the platform, Conservation, Islam, Christianity, Housing, or Palm Oil Plantations, they all take credit for 'rescuing' the Orang Rimba. It is the same with WARSI and their conservation platform. The long-term results remain to be seen. Some groups provide ideas and approaches that could be beneficial but could also be harmful. Everything could be either completely right or totally wrong. Ha, even my own thinking might be completely wrong.

WARSI succeeded in enlarging the territory of Bukit Dua Belas to twice its original area (from 32,000 to 60,500 hectares), and changing its status from 'Biosphere Reserve' to 'National Park' in 2000. Currently its main agenda is to complete its field databases, collect information on natural resources, the distribution of Orang Rimba and other data, compiling this data into various maps.

From my limited perspective, there is something wrong with WARSI's premise of giving priority to saving the rainforest and by extension, also saving the Orang Rimba. Should the Orang Rimba be active in supporting rainforest conservation? If the answer is "no", then there is no natural partnership between WARSI and the Orang Rimba. What happens to a rainforest conservation program without the support of the community living in the rainforest?

I cannot bear to see the Orang Rimba put in a position where they have no room to maneuver. Once cornered, they will have no capacity to objectively assess problems coming their way. On a more pro-active note, I would like the Orang Rimba to have a say in their future destiny, and to do so they need to be empowered.

For me, therefore, this is not just about rainforest conservation. It is also about the survival of the Orang Rimba. I realize that my personal attachment to this place is not because of the rainforest, but because of the people. Yet, that does not mean I care any less about their habitat.

I come to the conclusion that reading and writing alone is not adequate preparation for the Orang Rimba to chart their future. Obviously, just having a Butet around is not enough. Even if I sacrifice myself, it still won't be enough. I realize that I cannot fight this alone. In order to meet their needs, I must seek help from others.

Education needs to take sides (surprise, surprise).

I learn that many Orang Rimba have begun to clear land for rubber and vegetable cultivation. Teaching agro-forestry might add value to their existing local knowledge. What other training do they need? Where do they report the theft of lumber from their rainforest? I realize they may need to become familiar with the law, their basic human rights and other similar subjects.

I also realize they need their own voice to be heard. Some have expressed the desire to share their knowledge of the rainforest with the outside world. Others would like to write about rainforests for newspapers, although their writing skills are not yet up to the standard required for publication. I think some knowledge about printed media might help. First, they need the skills to voice their opinions in writing, in a newspaper article, and then they need some knowledge of using printed media for campaign purposes.

What about art? Although it is common in the 'other world' to suppose that the Orang Rimba have no appreciation of art, I feel that they can communicate their thoughts, fears and feelings through art.

They can experiment with different media, for example, sculpting with wood or clay, pencil drawing, or using other materials around them. Hmmm . . . I need assistance teaching this. The ideal would be to find someone who is willing to experiment in the outdoors.

Uh, so much to do! But how do I start? I have neither the financial means, nor the people.

This dream of my ideal education model keeps recurring. Every time I settle on one idea, another seemingly more effective one comes to light. This happens regularly, even after several years. It started when I left WARSI, then when I was writing this book in Yogyakarta, and again during my preparation to teach reading and writing in East Timor.

These thoughts keep pulling me back to the rainforests of Jambi. I miss the children's puppy-faced expressions and their laughter.

Whatever will happen to them? If I stop now, I will surely regret it later. By then it will be too late. I am certain that a school tailored to the daily needs of the Rimba and held on their turf is essential for the children.

Meanwhile, WARSI clearly rejects the idea of developing the capacity of my Orang Rimba pupils, criticizing me for curriculum deviations. As far as I understand, the concept of conservation does not necessarily take into account the existence of humans in National Parks. Are National Parks supposed to be sterile places without human presence or activities? I assume that WARSI does not take my education plans seriously because, given their conservation agenda, the forest is more important than the Orang Rimba.

What about me? I want to be content with the things that I have done in the last four years at WARSI. At the moment, I feel like I am giving ice cream to a little child. However, in my case, the child is blindfolded and can only have one lick. Or maybe it is more like giving a boy a fishing rod without teaching him how to fish. Even worse, I point him to a river that has no fish. Everything is half-done. Instead of empowering the children, the little knowledge I have given them burdens their hearts. Once they are able to read, they become aware of their issues. Then they become depressed when they realize they are unable to defend their own rights.

Once they learn to read, the Orang Rimba become avid readers. From magazines, they learn of similar fates suffered by fellow tribal peoples in other places. From news reports, they learn about the law, and know that illegal logging is a punishable offense.

At the same time, illegal loggers are still quite free to roam around. It must hurt to be a spectator of your own people's decline, unable to do anything about it? Would it be better to be ignorant? What you don't know doesn't hurt you, after all. Is ignorance in this case a blessing? No, it is even more frightening.

I feel responsible for what I have already started. I also feel this is my calling, my duty. I can neither be angry with myself, nor stay quiet any more.

Suddenly I hear a loud voice, "What's the matter, Butet? When did you stop being neutral?"

Other voices interrupt, "Eh, who says you cannot take sides? Education needs to take sides!"

"You must be on the children's side. You are an educator, not some ordinary record playing this or that!"

Chapter 2

SOKOLA is here

On September 30, 2003 at ten at night, five WARSI staff members held a meeting in the Director's office. Coincidentally, it was the anniversary of the 1965 attempted coup d'état in Indonesia. Indit, Dodi, Oceu, Willy and I all shared a similar restlessness. We met to see if we could find some common ground. We looked for a private room suitable for a closed-door meeting. As it turned out, the only one that fit our needs was the WARSI Director's office. We went inside and, in a defiant mood, locked the door for our meeting.

Indit, my roommate and a former journalist, chaired the meeting, or to use the more hip word, the 'brainstorming session'. She reiterated that we shared a set of common ideas—that education is the natural right of every ethnic group, and should not be limited to reading and writing. We knew we held a shared view and now we wanted to implement our vision. We believed that any new plan of action should be extended to other indigenous communities in other parts of the country.

In the end, we agreed that we could no longer stay with WARSI if we wanted to realize our ambitions. We needed to create a new institution solely focused on education, and we had to start from scratch.

The meeting moved on to how to plan and form this new institution. We thought we could begin our education program at Bukit Tiga Puluh because we already knew the area well and WARSI did not operate there. We believed we could help the Orang Rimba there with literacy, numeracy and other educational needs. Naturally, we needed funds to run the program; our estimate was one to two million rupiah a month (around US$240 in 2003).

We didn't need the multi-billion rupiah budgets that funded NGO programs in some other provinces. We would establish an education program based on local culture using local resources. We would not need international consultants for needs assessments and monitoring, nor would we hire experts on endangered plants and animals to help us achieve our goals.

To raise the funds, Indit proposed publishing our experiences. We could include the Rimba children's education experiences, their paintings, photos, and sketches. Money raised from the sale of our books could be used to kick-start the program. The meeting was adjourned with an agreement that we would start preparing an education program for Bukit Tiga Puluh and simultaneously, start preparing materials for the book. We decided to meet again in three months to discuss next steps. We also decided to leave WARSI once the program material was developed and the book was ready for printing. We would play it safe to avoid starvation!

The following day, the 1st of October, I placed my letter of resignation on the director's desk. Hmmm . . . even though I had agreed with my colleagues not to be hasty, I could not stand it anymore. I had been thinking about these issues for such a long time, and had been holding back my objections for two years. The idea of starting a new institution inspired my confidence and motivated me to resign as soon as possible. There was no reason to force myself to linger any longer, to stay in a place where my voice was not heard, to follow the WARSI way of doing things. So I pioneered the "rebellion" and instigated a coup d'état.

For me, leaving WARSI was the best decision. I didn't see eye-to-eye with the group anymore and we were constantly in conflict over project details. My continued presence would only be a hindrance for them. If I did not like my job but stayed for the sake of a salary, I felt that I was prostituting my principles and myself. I wanted to be with the Orang Rimba in the rainforest, but at the same time, the Orang Rimba were suffering through the "nature conservation education" I conducted.

Honestly, when I first agreed to take up the assignment, I was not fully aware of how fundamental the differences were between my own and WARSI's views on the education program for the Orang Rimba. And over time I had changed my stand as I came to a greater understanding of the issues and no longer believed in the validity of the WARSI education program.

The first thing I did after leaving WARSI was to look for new lodgings. Clearly, I couldn't stay in WARSI housing any longer, but I needed to stay on in Jambi. Fortunately, my good friend, Wir, was happy to shelter me temporarily. My mother (who coincidentally had come to Jambi to do some office work for two weeks) and I packed up all my belongings and moved me to Wir's house.

Once the move was complete, I immediately returned to Bukit Dua Belas to visit my students. There was a moment of anxiety. Was this going to be my last visit? I thought, "Hmmm . . . whatever happens will happen." I knew for certain that whatever future obstacles arose, I would not let them separate me from my students. I went to Kejasung Besar and Makekal Hulu to meet my trainees. This time in the jungle, I lived like Tarzan. There were neither equipment nor provisions from Bangko. I ate whatever the Orang Rimba ate.

When I saw my students I told them that it was going to be different from now on. I could not help out with either food or writing materials because I was no longer employed by WARSI and I did not earn a salary anymore. I wanted to continue teaching them. I asked them, "Will you feed me?" They answered, "Of course, as long as you are happy to eat whatever is in our daily harvest."

I stayed with the Orang Rimba for two months and I felt a tremendous sense of liberty. The air felt soothing. I moved and taught without the pressure of having to reach a certain number of students. The program followed the rhythm of the Orang Rimba's life. It was very pleasant, but this contentment had its price. I had depleted all my savings. There was only a little money left to buy the cheap portable computer I needed to assemble the material for this book.

I went straight to Jakarta after leaving the Rimba and spent several weeks at my mother's home. I went to Yogyakarta in an attempt to start writing. Writing while traveling between Jakarta and Yogyakarta (more than 500 kilometers away) was difficult and exhausting. After two months, the outline of the book was still in chaos, and the writing a shambles. Physically I was working on the book, but my thoughts were always with my Rimba students.

During this time, I met two journalists from Gerbang magazine, an education periodical interested in covering school activities in the Rimba. They wanted to visit the Rimba with me. I suggested they contact WARSI directly because I had resigned from the organization. They should meet WARSI's new education facilitator, my replacement. They insisted that I go with them because they thought that I had pioneered the Rimba education system. They even tried unsuccessfully to ask their boss to fund my travel when they found out I didn't have any money for the trip. Meeting them was a cathartic release and I felt a strong urge to go back to the Rimba. "*Ya*, Butet, you should not let anything stop you now!" I told myself.

I scraped the bottom of the barrel for my last few rupiah and with donations from my younger brother and mother, I left for Jambi with the two Gerbang journalists in a rented car. We drove to the edge of the rainforest. The rest of the journey was on foot, walking to the *rombong* of Bekilat at *rombong Temenggung* Mirak and Makekal Hulu. For about a year, this *rombong* had been my regular transit spot. We walked for two hours and by the time we arrived at *rombong* Bekilat, it was already dusk. Bekilat could not believe his eyes when he saw us. His eyes gleamed when he saw me. Apparently the news of my leaving WARSI had spread to all the *rombong* within the Bukit Dua Belas Park and they didn't think that I would return to the Rimba.

"*Astaga! Ibu Guru* is here!! How are you, old girl?"

My fatigue melted away as I heard the familiar cheeky greetings. Later, Asep and Mahli, the two journalists, said that I looked happy but also sad when I met the Orang Rimba. When they saw how much I missed being in the Rimba and teaching to my heart's content, they voluntarily covered my expenses, right up to our return to Jambi.

Having collected enough material for their article, the three of us went to Jambi accompanied by Bekilat and Peniti Benang. Once in Jambi, the two journalists went their own way and Bekilat, Peniti Benang, and I continued our journey to Bukit Tiga Puluh. We planned to do a feasibility study to see what kind of school we could establish in the Rimba.

In Jambi, we waited at the bus terminal on our way to *Dusun* Tuo Ilir and then Bukit Tiga Puluh. It was eleven in the morning, the bus had not yet appeared and we had been waiting since dawn. I felt pangs of hunger but tried to suppress them. To lower my expenditures to save money for my return trip to Jakarta, I had replaced my three meals per day with two. Meanwhile, Peniti Benang and Bekilat, who were also hungry, bought some *ketoprak*. They told me that I should eat too, but I refused. They looked at me for a long time and knew that my refusal was not due to lack of hunger.

"Just eat, *Ibu*, we will pay for it!" they said.

I was moved and could not look at them. While eating, I nearly burst into tears. I was so irritated with my helpless situation. If even feeding myself was a struggle, how could I start an educational program without any financial backing?

We left soon after midday and finally reached the village Tuo Ilir after dark. We took refuge overnight at a food vendor's stall. I knew him from previous visits and he was surprised to hear that I had left WARSI. We left the following morning to travel to the Batang Hari River, which we crossed on a big raft. We passed several Orang Rimba from Bukit Tiga Puluh whom I knew from previous visits. They told me that some *rombong* were planning to go to Riau within the next two weeks to collect rattan in order to make enough money to cultivate their land. When we arrived, we saw that the Orang Rimba were indeed occupied with the work of moving so we decided to stay only for one night. After that, we returned to Bukit Dua Belas.

Back in Jakarta, I started to have doubts. My enthusiasm began to wane. I felt alone and started to lose my confidence. Would I be able to achieve anything by myself, without any financial backing? Four months had passed since we had our first discussions about the formation of a new organization. Nothing had happened since then.

The situation, in fact, had worsened. We hardly communicated and there was no follow up after our first enthusiastic meeting. Some of the original five were still with WARSI. They continued complaining, so why didn't they leave? Dodi and Indit left WARSI in November 2003, soon after I did. Dodi took up a mainstream position in a company with his older sister, while Indit continued her Master's studies at the University of Indonesia. I was hesitant to contact them, just in case they had changed their minds.

Meanwhile, I became increasingly disheartened, feeling lethargic and losing interest in my surroundings. I did not feel like searching for a job. Anything to do with Orang Rimba education, I pushed to the back of my mind, and tried to forget. I was in denial; I could not carry out what I aspired to do. I could neither raise funds, nor rally any support from friends. Every time I brought up the subject with other people, they looked at me with pity, and tried to divert my interest to other things. I prepared for a new project, offered to me by INSIST Foundation, teaching reading and writing in East Timor. This was my only hope; it was similar to my old work, but it was funded. I also had to continue writing as I had won a one-year grant from INSIST to write my book.

Thank God, in the midst of this despair, I saw a light at the end of the tunnel. In January 2004, Stefanie, a friend from Germany who had visited the Rimba in 2002, contacted me. She wanted to go back to the Rimba for her anthropology PhD research project, a project that would take two years. Her arrival gave me a flicker of hope. As soon as I heard her plan, I immediately offered my services as guide, porter and translator. Of course, my main objective was to return to the Orang Rimba.

During our time together, I recounted my experiences and all the related complexities. She respected my dreams and encouraged me to not give up. She even tried to foster my ideas by putting them into a program proposal. She looked up acquaintances in Indonesia to canvas for support, and my hope grew stronger.

When Stefani and I were in the middle of the project proposal, Dodi and Indit joined us. I was very pleased and welcomed them. My previous hesitancy had been unjustified. Dodi had left a lucrative career, and Indit, although burdened with the demands of her studies, did her best to help us in whatever ways she could.

I realized, though we never talked about it, that their actions spoke volumes, making up for any doubts I thought they had about our mission. Likewise, I owed them an apology for doubting their commitment and spirit. Our torch, or more precisely our flame of hope, had been lit again.

In March 2004, I received the Woman of the Year award from ANTV, a national broadcasting company based in Jakarta. The award included a stipend of twenty million rupiah (about US$2,000). I was ecstatic, and thought the money could be spent on the education program for the Orang Rimba. I was able to travel back and forth from the Rimba without having to depend on my stipend because I was Stefani's guide.

In April 2004, Oceu and Willy resigned from WARSI. Our group was finally complete, the "unemployed intellectual bunch" could now go to work for ourselves.

Around the same time, a foundation, Global Environmental Facilities—Small Grant Program responded to our project proposal. They asked us to work out a new, more complete and systematic proposal as our original proposal was vague in parts. We were unsure about what to include or how to express our ideas in a systematic fashion. The proposal we submitted was actually a plan of activities. We simply sought expressions of interest to gauge possible reactions.

Fortunately, the GEF director, Avi, was willing to assist us with refining the proposal. Doctor Ati (who worked with me in the Rimba 2000-2002, resigned in 2002 and now worked with an international NGO) donated some money to be used as start-up capital.

When we finished the proposal, we sent it out again without a clue as to whether it would have any impact. While waiting for a reply, we worked through and expanded our ideas and established SOKOLA, an educational organization supplying field solutions in remote locations.

We strengthened our group by including several friends. I asked Rubby, a keen nature lover I had met in Surabaya during environmental education training, to join us. He was studying at the Institute for Teachers Training and Education and had visited the Rimba in 2002, after saving for a whole year for the trip. I noticed that he had a great talent for teaching and the children liked him very much. I had previously recommended him to be WARSI's education facilitator, but they felt he did not have the required qualifications. He was very pleased when we asked him to join our activities in the Rimba. "Awesome! Joining crazy people like you guys," he said. When I met him in Jambi, I found out that he had recently left university for financial reasons.

We also sought the assistance of a nurse named Hani. I met her at a nature lover's club called PALAWA UNPAD. She expressed interest in being involved for three months and wanted to teach the Orang Rimba about health. She ended up being in the jungle for three years and continues our program in Aceh.

In all, our SOKOLA group came to seven: Dodi the anthropologist, Oceu the painter, Indit the media campaign expert, Willy the surveyor and map expert, Rubby the environmental education expert, Hani the nurse and me.

By July, we began to put our program into practice and to realize our goals. Our start-up funds included the money left over from my award, some additional donations, and everything we found when we turned our pockets inside out. We planned to invest more funds throughout the year, but that would not materialize for months. We then sold most of our belongings (except our pride, he he he) to augment our coffers. We entered the Rimba and headed to Bukit Dua Belas where we initially worked, not to Bukit Tiga Puluh. The fact that WARSI was not working in Bukit Tiga Puluh was not a strong enough "pull" to begin our project there. We had worked in Bukit Dua Belas before, and we felt it would be an easier transition to start there again.

The first order of business was to develop an education program for the Orang Rimba students that raised their existing skill levels and created alternatives for their future. We believed the rainforest was not the only means of making a living for the Orang Rimba. The focus on rainforest conservation at any cost was the domain of the conservationists. Of course, we would like to save the rainforest, but what if we could not? One of my students had said, "It is ok for you *Ibu guru*, because if the rainforest is depleted, you only have to go home to your village and live with your mother. But what about us, where will we go? There will be nothing for us even to eat here."

Rimba youth are concerned about issues of income diversification as well as maintaining their local traditions. To ensure a source of income, we thought that the students who reach adolescence should become role models for the younger students. This idea was modeled on the practice used by Rimba parents to pass down rainforest responsibilities to the next generation. Our older students would like to have cultivation plots and learn to plant and harvest them. At the same time, these plots would deter the thrust of land clearance by the village people.

The students said, "This is the real school, learning how to live and have a good life." This saying became the basis for SOKOLA. SOKOLA contributes to matters related to daily living and prepares people to deal with the onslaught of new experiences brought on by changing times. The rainforest is diminishing and the Orang Rimba are already becoming integrated with the market system. If there are well protected rainforests and the Orang Rimba are able to be completely self-sufficient within them, without any market exchange with the outside world, we might assume that they would not need schooling. However, all the evidence points to the contrary.

We came up with the idea of a boarding school where children stay at school and away from their parents. The school would provide everything and all activities would be done there. Every day would be a school day and daily life would center on the school. And so, school would no longer be just books and pencils. Naturally, the children would be allowed to visit their parents, especially those children beginning to shoulder family responsibilities.

We began to expand our curriculum to include knowledge of flora and fauna. We dissected a frog to show its respiratory and digestive systems. We stressed however that only frogs could be subjected to this exercise. The children had joked, rather alarmingly, about experimenting on the oldest person in the rainforest, dissecting him and sewing him up again. If he didn't survive, well, not much would be lost. *Wah* . . . so disrespectful!

We also took the children to attend Orang Rimba's *adat* meetings. All of us, the children, my colleagues and I took notes during the proceedings. We learned how the elders subtly created rhymes to convey their messages or to share their feelings.

We encouraged the children to speak up and express themselves in open forums. If a government official was present, the children tended to whisper among themselves, too timid to stand up. Here we would encourage them saying, *"Pak, this is Pengendum and he has something to say."* We set them up to talk, which otherwise wouldn't have happened. If Pengendum sulked, we would deal with it later.

We often invited the Rimba elders to chat with us at SOKOLA. Through casual chatting, the children picked up knowledge and guidance from the elders' life experiences. The children asked about legends, spells, traditional medicine, ghosts, mythology and a myriad of other things, some of which I didn't quite understand. These *adat* elders became our teachers. Although some of our questions may have sounded silly to their ears, the elders were generally pleased to pass on their knowledge, validating their esteemed place.

Apart from running the school, we also made the rounds visiting each of the Orang Rimba homes. They were spread over great distances, anything from a ten-minute walk to a three-hour trek away. Occasionally, we would have sessions with the wider *rombong* group, depending on their issues. Usually, this was done at the request of the Orang Rimba. If the request was during the *melangun*, then we traveled with them.

Meanwhile journalists began to get wind of my activities, some regarded me as a strange creature anyway, and they started to contact me. I was urged by friends to take these opportunities to campaign about the Orang Rimba's predicament and to use their stories to raise awareness of the program. So, I made myself available to the journalists. Some media coverage resulted in fund-raising opportunities for SOKOLA; yet other media events needed contributions from us just to make them happen.

I was invited to speak at a university in Makassar. They had a good program concept, but were short of funds. So, I coughed up the cost of the trip to be able to participate and share my experiences with them. *Ya*, naturally, we didn't expect too much financial assistance from this sort of academic activity.

Fortunately, in November 2004, after nearly a year with no funding, financial assistance from the foundation was ready for disbursement. Finally, we had solid financial backing for our program, having relied solely on our private means since July when my award money had run out.

The school activities and ambience had changed a great deal since my time at WARSI. Now, we took turns cooking and collecting wood and we slept in the same hut. None of the teacher trainees received payment for assisting with teaching. Likewise, there was no money involved when the children served as guides or porters when they accompanied a visitor to another part of the Rimba. I felt my relationship with the Orang Rimba was now more sincere and honest. The Rimba children were very happy studying here.

The younger children idolized the teacher trainees. They used the word *"melawon"* to express their admiration. This is the equivalent of being "cool". The trainees had a good command of Indonesian and could hold their own when communicating with the outside world.

They also had friends in the outside world who would journey to Jakarta and speak on behalf of the Orang Rimba and the rainforest.

The students began to comprehend and acquire some of the ways of the outside world, yet they remained comfortable with their own customs. They were skilled at different methods of animal hunting and trapping, familiar with folk legends and spells. If asked by someone from the outside world about their aspirations, their answer would be, "to be a teacher trainee." Despite this optimistic picture, the situation for the Rimba did not represent total freedom of opportunity. A career as head of a political party or as governor seemed unlikely for any of our pupils.

As time passed and we progressed with SOKOLA in Bukit Dua Belas, several disturbing incidents took place that inevitably re-connected me with WARSI. Apparently several students from Bukit Dua Belas felt my absence over the seven months I was in 'exile' at Bukit Tiga Puluh. These loyal students, Bekilat, Peniti Benang, Pengendum, and Pemilang Laman, expressed their discontent by being disruptive to WARSI. They did things that they knew would upset WARSI staff. They asked journalists in Bangko to publish articles about their concerns about their future and their disappointment with WARSI. They said that WARSI contributed very little to the preservation of the Bukit Dua Belas rainforest, their habitat.

In the end, I was accused of urging the students to do this. *Astaganaga* . . . worm of all worms, I am not that cruel. Besides I was at Bukit Tiga Puluh the entire time and had no contact with the Bukit Dua Belas students. The situation became worse when a journalist interviewed and filmed the students, then took the results to WARSI. He blackmailed WARSI saying that if they did not pay, he would sell the film to one of the television stations. WARSI refused to pay and persuaded the journalist to change his mind. Ah, I was vexed. I knew the journalist. How did he have the heart to try to profit from this situation?

In 2010, SOKOLA became a legal entity. It spread its activities to other provinces: Makassar, Aceh, Flores and the Moluccas. Due to our financial limitations, some of these programs have been forced to close down. We also conducted short sessions after the earthquakes in areas such as Garut, Cianjur, Yogyakarta, Klaten and West Sumatra.

As we expanded our activities, we needed additional personnel. However, recruitment was severely constrained by a lack of funds. There were a lot of things we didn't fully consider in our business plan. For example, we did not include activities related to the development of our funding base. Many programs would take off and expand. To meet the constant demand for new SOKOLA teachers, we resorted to recruiting volunteers through word-of-mouth via friends, letters and emails. We called this recruitment method "*mandiri* volunteer recruitment", *mandiri* meaning independent.

This meant that volunteers had to come up with their own funds for going to the location, knowingly taking the risk of malaria, wild animal attacks, illness and even the chance of getting lost in the jungle. We provided only accommodations and food. For us, providing accommodations meant, "There are plenty of trees and leaves, here is a machete, build your own house!" And for food, we pointed to the speedy fawn and said, "There is your food, go after it!" He he he . . . no, we were not that cruel, but almost.

Amazingly, we had more recruits than we needed. Our group blossomed from seven to twenty-six people. None, however, had the privileged assurance of a regular salary, health insurance or any other employment benefits. We were doing our best to find ways to fund these benefits, so far without result. Not that they demanded what was due to them. They said that they were happy to make their social contribution for the betterment of these people, as long as they could still eat.

I realized that we were operating in an unprofessional way. We still had a lot to learn and we had the future to think about. I was playing a part in putting twenty-six people's future livelihoods at risk. Each time I arrived at our "office" in my family's home in Jakarta, my mother commented, "Who is this, your latest victim?"

Chapter 3

Rimba bound

We are perplexed about how to respond to people who ask for our address in the jungle. There are no villages or *rombong* boundaries here. We don't even know our precise location in relation to a village or within a province. We do know the geographic location of SOKOLA—01° 50′ South, 102° 30′ East. This is our address if anyone would like to send us letters . . . he he he. As for email, we are so isolated we would have to use carrier pigeons to pass on messages!

Today, the city of Jambi feels hotter than usual, although it is early in the morning and dry and dusty. I still find it a pleasant change, having been away for such a long time. Recently, I have been traveling helter-skelter around Aceh, Flores and Makassar running the SOKOLA program. We are still short of personnel, even though we have new recruits. SOKOLA locations in the Bukit Dua Belas Park are also still growing, which means we need even more teaching staff in Jambi, which is under Willy's co-ordination.

We are focusing on the concept of school centers to cater to the dispersed and changing pattern of Orang Rimba *rombong* locations. Each center focuses on a different program, depending on the education needs of the surrounding Orang Rimba. Some place environmental study, agriculture and forestry at their core, while others concentrate on reading and writing.

In Jambi, the prospect of returning to the jungle is very exciting for me. I cannot deny my emotional attachment to the rainforest. I have a constant longing to be there. This time, the return journey to the jungle feels arduous and long, straining my patience. Yet, I am eager to see the children.

It takes six hours by public transport to travel the 220 km distance from Jambi to Bangko. The road is severely pot-holed, which adds to the agony of the trip. Plus, I have a headache, listening to local folk songs transformed into a strange kind of house music, blaring at maximum volume. Under normal circumstances, the folk music would be quite enjoyable. I recognize the songs because they are quite popular in this area. Now I just feel sick looking at the interior of the minibus and hearing the music. I stuff my ears with pieces of tissue.

I arrive at Bangko in the late afternoon. With a tiny population compared to Jakarta, the city is calm and pleasant. It is quite likely everybody knows everybody here. I myself know a number of people in Bangko, having been in and around the area for the last six years. Still, from time to time, people ask me, "Where are you from?" Normally I answer in a cheeky way, "From the market, *Pak*."

The next day I travel by *ojek*, a motorbike taxi, to the village of Bungo Tanjung adjacent to the Transmigration Settlement on the western side of the National Park, around 35 kilometers from Bangko. I need to go further to the Makekal River on the western side of Bukit Dua Belas where the headquarters of SOKOLA is located.

The journey on the motorbike is far more enjoyable than that on the minibus. I am used to riding a motorbike by myself when going into the jungle now. Thinking back, I grin wryly remembering how SOKOLA's pet Honda was repossessed by the dealer because we could not make the installment payments.

When traveling I usually disguise myself as a stout man, stuffing my jacket for effect, wearing gloves, boots, and a closed helmet. This camouflage helps me feel secure and sort of cool as well. Disguising myself as a man, however, does not always guarantee my safety.

When I was working for WARSI several years ago, I had an accident while driving their trail bike with Bekilat. We were carrying two huge backpacks which we tied to the back of the motorbike. It was raining hard and we slipped and fell on a muddy, rough and rocky road in between some palm oil plantations. Some motorists stopped and approached us. The motorbike and backpacks were heaped on top of us. In a panic, they touched us to see if we were still breathing. Some of their hands got too close for comfort. "Are you ok, son?" one of the strangers asked me.

"Who are you calling son? Hands off me!" I thought to myself. I nearly punched the man. However, I kept quiet. I casually brushed away his hands. It turned out that my left calf was scorched from contact with the motorbike engine. It smelled like roast beef . . . mm mm, yummy . . . but it hurt really badly. I felt compelled to suppress the pain for fear of more unwanted contact. The minute the other motorists left, I hollered and cried in pain.

Bekilat laughed at my disguise for the rest of the journey. Not only did it not protect me from injury, it did nothing to save me from strangers' hands checking for broken bones. However, I do like the scar that the accident left, it looks like a fish catching a worm.

"Traveling by yourself, *Ibu*?" the *ojek* driver interrupts my daydream. I say casually, "My friends are already there." I tell a little white lie because a woman traveling alone is still uncommon in this area and has a negative connotation.

It is dusk when I ride past the villages and the rubber plantation. It occurs to me momentarily that my driver might be a thug, but I brush off the thought. I feel for my commando knife strapped to my calf. Ah, it is still there. I smile quietly, fancying myself a female James Bond. I don't even know how to use a knife to defend myself. I use it for chopping firewood and chili peppers.

As I enter the Bungo Tanjung village, I am overwhelmed to see the changes. Ohh . . . this village has developed so much. There are more shops at *Pasar Selasa* or Tuesday Market, so named because it only operates on Tuesdays. At the edge of town, I notice an out-of-place, imposing green house with a high fence. Next door are rows of barracks-like houses, possibly to lodge the people who work for the owner of the grand house. It must be the residence of Bedul Kayo, a well-known wealthy local, possibly one of the richest men in Jambi. His wealth must have quadrupled since I last visited the area. His name, Bedul Kayo, is a mystery to me. No one seems to know his real name. "Maybe his name is Abdul," say several villagers when I ask them. Everyone has nicknamed him Bedul Kayo, a strange nickname because *bedul* means stupid and *kayo* means rich.

Apparently Bedul Kayo is illiterate. He is in his fifties, and the owner of a number of bulldozers, road rollers and an off-road four-wheel-drive Ford Ranger (my dream car, he he he), not to mention tens of trucks, hundreds or maybe thousands of hectares of rubber plantations and 400 workers to tap the sap. His rubber plantations run nine kilometers on either side of the primary road in this area. From the edge of the road, the plantations also run for tens of kilometers inland. Rumor has it that all this is not from some generous inheritance or gift. Bedul Kayo started out as a fishmonger at the market.

Lots of questions pop into my mind about the rainforest. What is it like now? Has anything changed? I have kept up with developments through my colleagues from the SOKOLA team as well as from one or two students who communicate with me via telephone when they come out of the jungle. Nevertheless, I still feel unsure about the challenges that might be ahead for our SOKOLA.

At the outskirts of the village, I am taken by surprise at the extensive road development. It resembles the veins of a leaf. The Orang Rimba recently told me that there are already two roads penetrating the Bukit Dua Belas National Park and that one ends about 300 meters from the hut of Pengendum, one of my pupils at Napu River. The other road from Sako Jernang River is about two kilometers long.

I know that the effect of the roads is not entirely positive. Nevertheless, I also realize that no matter how convinced I am about certain matters, it does not necessarily mean that development like this is wrong. Take the clearing of the jungle for the road, for example. The Orang Rimba themselves agreed to the extension of the road to enable Bedul Kayo's cars to go as far as possible into the interior. This way, the Orang Rimba do not have to travel so far to transport their rubber, *damar* (resin) or rattan. Obviously, this is not the case for all Orang Rimba. I am only aware of this happening on the western side of the National Park.

It does not stop here. I hear more stories. The latest fad among the Orang Rimba is the motorbike. Several Orang Rimba have sold land to buy motorbikes. A villager must arrange for the purchase because Orang Rimba do not have identity cards, which are required for an official purchase of a vehicle. The Orang Rimba do not have identity cards because one of the requirements is to state one's religion from the list of national religions, and their religion is not listed.

There are instances where Orang Rimba have just exchanged a plot of land for a used motorbike. Sometimes the installment payments on the loan for the bike have not all been made yet. The motorbike dealer then chases them down to collect the rest of the installments. There is one particular case, which I found hard to believe, but it turned out to be true. An Orang Rimba bought a motorbike just to admire and polish it because he did not know how to ride it.

I become increasingly worried. It is clear that much of the land that was sold is on the outskirts of the National Park while some is located right inside the Park. This means that outsiders can now expand their land rights into the interior of the rainforest. It also means that the livelihood of the Orang Rimba is under threat. Hmm . . . am I right? Or am I just being overly dramatic?

One thing is clear. The Orang Rimba's way of life is being directly challenged by the changing times. I ask myself whether this change means that they are no longer dependent on the rainforest? Are they content to move into a house or to join the elbowing, nudging, competitive city folks? My skin crawls. It terrifies me just imagining it, especially since people's perceptions of the Orang Rimba have not changed very much. The villagers still call the Orang Rimba *"Kubu"*.

After passing another village, we approach the edge of the jungle. We stop and I jump off the motorbike. I pick up my backpack and look around. It doesn't look at all like the rainforest I remember from my last visit. The surroundings feel different but I can't be sure because I don't know this particular spot well. I continue walking, following the pathway into the jungle. Unexpectedly, having only trekked for twenty minutes, I see huts and several Orang Rimba. I have already arrived at the SOKOLA center!

Unbelievable! How did this happen? I haven't yet worked up a sweat; this was like a short trip to the paddy field. I am right. The jungle has been cleared, reducing the distance from the rainforest's edge to the huts, which would have previously been in the deep interior of the tropical forest.

How disturbing. The last time I visited, it took me more than 40 minutes to walk here. Two years ago, the walk took one hour and five years ago it took two days to walk here from the last village and the jungle was so dense we got lost. Now, I can hear the sound of motorbikes from my hut. I complain about this to my colleagues, but they remain silent. They also remember how much time it used to take to reach the next school center at *Temenggung* Mirak. Previously, it took them five hours. Now, it only takes two because the Bedul Kayo Road reaches the Sako Napu River.

Where will these changes lead? Should we re-focus our education objectives? Can changes brought by the outside world be avoided? Do we fight these changes or just go along with them? Given the rate of change, I realize now that we are racing against time. We must push to continue studying and striving so that we can cope with this new future. It is like developing anti-viruses for computers, forever chasing one's tail.

Plunk! Suddenly a snake lands on the ground, skimming my head. I shriek in fear. It stares at me equally dumbfounded, regains its bearings and prepares to attack. I should stand there calmly and breathe normally but my strong sense of self-preservation kicks in and in self-defense, I flee. I sprint and jump up into a hut. Pemilang Laman intervenes and kills the offending poisonous green snake. Ah, poor thing, why did he have to die? He just fell accidentally. Hmm . . . at least this indicates that there is wildlife here and this place can still be called a jungle. I console myself with this thought.

Recovered from the shock, I head to the Makekal River. I submerge myself in the water as I normally do. It is not a very pretty river but at least its water is clear. I have fallen into this river so many times. Its riverbed is rather unique and called *napol* by the Orang Rimba. *Napol* is a word to describe a creviced, uneven, grey cement-like river floor, firm but moldable if pressed with the fingertips. We frequently dig up this riverbed for clay, using it to sculpt various figures.

Once, the children made a hand phone and a camera out of the river clay. Then, they pretended to use the telephone and posed in front of the camera. *Waduh* . . . they must get these ideas from watching me! I use a mobile phone to communicate with the outside world. If I want to make a call, I walk up a hill called *Bukit Setan* (Devil's Hill) where I can receive a signal. It takes one hour by foot to reach *Bukit Setan* from the school.

The Rimba children call the hill *Bukit Setan* because they often observe us acting strangely when we are up there. It looks as though we are possessed: smiling, laughing, looking sad or even dancing around, all with the mobile phone against our ear. When they first saw our strange behavior, they said, "Yes, it is true what my friends say, it is indeed a Devil's Hill."

The fact that we need to carry a machete or other weapon when we go up Devil's Hill adds to the reputation of the area. The weapons are a precaution. Many bears roam around the area because it is packed with *puwor* trees and bears love the fruit.

Taking a bath in the river is my most pleasurable pastime. I know precisely where the crevice of the "bath tub" is located. I can laze around in this spot and just enjoy whiling the time away, pretending to be invisible. Sometimes little baby shrimp swim around and nip my skin. I often catch them when they are not on guard and then release them. I imagine them cursing as they run away.

There are also small frogs that swim in front of me as they try to cross the river. I am always tempted to catch them too, but it is not easy. One day, I succeeded in catching one. It reminded me of the well-known tale, and I proceeded to kiss it. Oh, it did not transform into a prince. I grinned at my own silliness. The frog jumped quickly away, pleased or angry I am not sure, "wok . . . wok . . . wok," he said.

I feel relaxed immersed in the cool water. I close my eyes enjoying the gentle flow of the water. But my mind cannot stop working, jumping from thought to thought. All the unexpected events during this journey upset me. Ah, sometimes I feel as if I am facing a brick wall.

We labor to keep SOKOLA running while time keeps ticking. Just look at the physical condition of the school. It is in a rickety, dilapidated state. We have four huts here: one for teachers and trainees, one for the students, one for the school and the last for the kitchen.

When I arrive, I notice that the hut for studying is collapsing. They tell me this is because the roof was built too tightly, making it susceptible to rot when the rain comes. And the teacher's hut, it will only take someone leaning on a pillar before it collapses. We decide to demolish the two huts and use the material left over to build a new place. In practice, we actually don't need four huts. We can study just about anywhere. It's the same with cooking and sleeping. Our huts are not pretty but we, and especially the children, are very proud of the school. There is nothing to be ashamed of. Moreover, who is here to make us feel ashamed? He he he.

A friend visits SOKOLA. He shakes his head seeing the state of our school. Naturally, he is shocked as he came with the usual expectations of a school including regular starting and finishing times, division of classes by student age, uniforms, report cards and so on. He expects a school building with a picture of the President, or a model of a human skeleton in the corner or a flagpole and bell in the middle of a playing field. He is surprised with what seems to be a lack of restraint in the children's behavior. For instance, in the middle of a teaching session a passing squirrel creates havoc. The teaching only resumes when the children recover from chasing the poor animal.

If the weather is good, we prefer to be outside in the open air, under the trees or by the banks of the river. We take walks with our books rolled up, our pens clipped to them or tucked into shorts or loincloths. We sometimes give lessons lying down. Sometimes the children have not washed for the whole day out of laziness. On some occasions, if I feel like it, I wear a cooling powder mask on my face. Once, when I had left some powder lying around, the children used the leftover facial mask powder for cooking, thinking it was ground pepper.

During his visit, my friend cannot get over the children's style of pointing at the blackboard with their feet. Or, when a child is being more courteous, his protruding lips reach toward the blackboard in the typical Orang Rimba style. Some children toss their book to the teacher in the midst of teaching, for correction. I explain to my visitor that, for the Orang Rimba, this is more practical than having the teacher wait for the book to be delivered by hand at the end of the lesson.

His only comment is, "What kind of school is this? What fun!" When we hear this, everybody looks at one another and says, "Sokola

Rimba!!" That is our school; full of the freedom that marks the Rimba culture.

There is only one hitch we have yet to overcome—the majority of our students are boys. From the beginning, there have only been six female students, all coming from a group that has more exposure to the outside world. We still have not succeeded in persuading any other Orang Rimba groups that their girls need an education too.

Our program is different from mainstream school programs because it is modified to suit the needs of the Orang Rimba. We can see this in the children's drawings. We do not find the usual depiction of the sun flanked by two triangular mountains that we often find in typical Indonesian students' drawings. The Rimba children don't usually draw landscapes, they draw the animals, birds and flowers they see every day. They have an eye for detail—they draw many different flowers with very specific petals and leaves.

I am always amazed at the imagination of these children! Any six year old will draw his father bravely chasing a boar or daringly depict a logger being bitten by a snake. They also draw ghosts and other creatures they see in their dreams. When I was a kid, I drew a house, a woman in a dress and, of course, those two typical mountains with the sun rising between them. Everything was frozen and boring; I never made a lively drawing telling a story. Why didn't I think to draw my brother's toothless grin, my nagging grandmother, or my father fixing the car?

Our school is not only concerned with drawing, writing and reading. We discuss the changes occurring within the Rimba, the increasingly high annual floods, the concept of "nation", the causes of tsunamis, or how airplanes (which the children call 'metal birds') fly. We often perform what would generally be regarded as laboratory experiments. We do not use that term because, in our case, all lessons are in our open laboratory, like the frog dissection. Admittedly, even our open laboratory has its limitations and we are sometimes caught unable to answer our pupils' more challenging questions.

My guest sees for himself our daily activities, which are a bit different from normal school activities. The students prepare hot drinks in the morning, tea or coffee with sugar or rainforest honey. They take a bath and, at the same time, wash the dishes from dinner the night before. And then, bursting with fresh energy and carrying their books in hand, they hang around their teacher who is still asleep, or purposely create a din to wake him or her up. There is no regular daily routine and there is always something new.

It is quite possible to spend the whole day playing in the jungle, searching for birds, squirrels, or fruit. Sometimes, the children set traps and check them from time-to-time for their catch. They attend *adat* meetings regularly. Some of the older boys have even started thinking seriously about their future.

Several boys start clearing land for the cultivation of rubber trees, and some plant rice, fruit, chili peppers and vegetables. They gather *damar* (resin) or sap from *jerenang* (rattan) also known as dragon's blood. They are skillful hunters. We often go hunting with them, joining just for the chase because we are more hindrance than help. Nonetheless, we are welcome to enjoy dining on the prey of the hunt.

Six youngsters in the school center show promise as teacher trainees. They started training when they were young and now work and teach in the rainforest. They hunt, accompanied by lean, formidable tracker dogs, and they have knowledge of spells and jungle mythology. Such are the boys' activities, as handed down from their fathers. As for the girls, they learn mat making from *rumbai* leaves, weave rattan baskets, collect roots and plants in the rainforest and fish.

From a very early age, Rimba children are trained to baby-sit younger children. They help collect firewood, fetch water from the river, wash the cooking utensils, and carry youngsters piggyback. It is not surprising to see six-year-olds deftly chopping firewood. They frequently laugh at my inept attempts to stack wood and light a fire. Even though I blow as hard as I can, the fire still will not light. The children are really extraordinary, and we learn a lot from them.

Once, Dodi, who is now the SOKOLA coordinator in Aceh, nodded in amazement listening to a seven-year-old explain how to set a trap for a fawn. It was a comical sight because Dodi is a wilderness survival instructor at Padjadjaran University. Another time, Willy naively followed the children's suggestion to cut down a particular tree. This type of tree causes itchiness and soreness. Despite the fact that Willy had been with the Rimba for seven years, he was still a novice among the children.

As for me, well, I get caught out by the children too. I cannot seem to learn to climb a tree and I have to wait for the help of little Berapit who climbs with great ease. On one occasion, he fetched a rope for me and tied it to the top of a SOKOLA hut. He climbed the tree by gripping his two miniscule legs around the trunk. He then stretched out and used the dangling rattan vine as a rope. Meanwhile, I just waited down below.

For some reason, I am still unable to climb a straight tree without branches, even when my life depends on it. I remember how, during my second year in the rainforest, I had great difficulty climbing a tree to escape from a bear.

I was with the children in the rainforest when they found that one of their traps had caught a bear cub. The older boys instinctively tried to kill it while driving the mother bear away. The younger children quickly climbed the tree. I was petrified. The tree was too slippery and as straight as a palm tree, so I kept sliding down. When the children looked down, they were shocked to see me slithering down instead of gaining height.

They started descending, grumbling, *"Aduh, Ibu guru* is still down there! How stupid! What a nuisance!" They quickly landed on the ground and gave a firm push to my behind until I reached a reasonably high branch. I felt stupid, an adult sitting in a tree with the small children, while the bigger kids were bravely trying to spear the bear cub. I could hear the bear cub shrieking in a panic, intense fear in its voice. I heard his heart-rending cries to his mother for help. I heard the sound of the mother in the distance, protesting angrily. The children responded with equal force to keep her at bay.

I could not contain myself anymore, and shouted. "That's enough! There is no need to kill the bear. Just let it go!" I was in tears. A small child in the next tree said softly, "Teacher, you cannot say that. The bear cub is a gift, and if the gods hear you, we won't be blessed with another gift next time." I nodded, digesting this. I hardened my heart telling myself that this is normal in the world of the Rimba. It was indeed the law of the jungle, natural and just.

I saw one child, perhaps it was Besemi, spear the bear cub in the chest. The bear caught the spear, bit it and broke it. Another student, Peniti Benang, commanded everyone to thrust their spears at once, ensuring that at least one would hit the target. The four children mounted a vigorous attack. Some successfully pierced the chest of the cub. He groaned and finally died. Then, I heard the mother bear. Her cry was angry at first, and then filled with despair. She slowly retreated away from us into the jungle. I could hear her cries fade as she moved further into the distance.

Oh, it is difficult to live with this! Especially later, when I join the feast. This is what survival means here, I realize, trying to visualize what would happen if our roles were reversed, if I was caught and devoured by a family of bears. I have received a most valuable lesson from the children. Life is hard in the natural course of things. Now, I try to view each situation within its context instead of from my own perspective.

A school curriculum must be designed according to the needs of its pupils, not from a template that has been approved by others. Even the best of intentions can flounder when we don't comprehend the needs of the intended recipients. The Orang Rimba would feel humiliated and hurt receiving what would be termed by the outside world as "donations" or "aid". It might be idealistic or heroic to the donors, but for the Orang Rimba, this aid is perceived as an insult. There are other repercussions of aid. The Orang Rimba are embarrassed by their nudity now that they have been given clothes to wear. They feel primitive and pitiful when they receive housing aid. It adds insult to injury when they are asked to convert from their religion.

Outside misconceptions play havoc with aid programs. Some think that the Orang Rimba will catch colds or fall ill if they don't live in a house with four walls. In reality, the most ideal and comfortable house for the Orang Rimba is one in which they can lie down with the soft wind caressing their faces and with the lullaby-like rustle of leaves serenading them to sleep. The jungle is their home, the place that means everything to the Orang Rimba.

Hmm, speaking of colds, I feel cold. I have been soaking in the river lost in my thoughts for too long. As I open my eyes, it is already dark. My body has started to shrivel. I set off in a hurry and head to my hut. I cannot afford to be away for too long because the children will be waiting. Their eyes will glimmer waiting for my stories.

I prepare myself by trying to remember everything. This is my first day back in the jungle after eight months away, and it has become a tradition that every time I return I have to share with them everything I have done while I was away.

And the story lives on . . .

Glossary

Word	Language	Definition
A		
adat	Indonesian	describes cultural norms, traditional laws, customary systems for dispute resolution, values, customs and traditional practices
Aduh!	Indonesian	an exclamation, like gee!
ambung	Rimba	rattan basket with straps, worn like backpack to carry various things. Available in smaller sizes to use for harvesting chili, fruits or fish and snails from the river
änjing penjilat burit	Rimba	bottom-licking dog, cleans the mess from babies' behinds
Astaga!	Indonesian	an exclamation, like gee whiz!
Astaganaga!	Indonesian	an exclamation. *Naga* is dragon, but is used as a rhyme for *astaga* simply to lengthen the exclamation.
au, au lah	Rimba	yes, yes of course
B		
bahasa	Indonesian	language
batagor	Indonesian	Sundanese Indonesian fried fish or meat and tofu croquette served with peanut sauce. Abbreviation for BAkso TAhu GOReng (meatball tofu fried)

Batak	Indonesian	collective term used to identify a number of ethnic groups predominantly found in North Sumatra, Indonesia. The stereotypical Batak person is straightforward, tough but with a melancholic personality.
batu	Indonesian	stone
becenenggo	Rimba	diseased
beik	Rimba	good, similar to Indonesian *baik*.
bejuku	Rimba	large tortoise
benor	Rimba	wild, edible tuber
bepak	Rimba	father
besasanding	Rimba	isolated to stop spread of infectious disease
Bu	Rimba	mother, also used as term of respect, ma'am. Similar to Indonesian *ibu*.
bubung, bubungon	Rimba	house, household
bukit, Bukit Dua Belas	Rimba	hill, Twelve Hills—a National Park
buku	Indonesian	book
bulan	Indonesian	month, moon
bungaron	Rimba	place for people who are healthy and unlikely to fall sick

D

damar	Rimba	resin produced by a tree named Dipterocarpaceae
dangdut	Indonesian	genre of Indonesian popular music with a distinct backbeat reminiscent of Bollywood

DAS	Indonesian	watershed, the land where rainwater runs downstream to a single reservoir or lake, abbreviation for Daerah Aliran Sungai
Datuk	Rimba	very old and respected man
dekat	Rimba	type of rambutan fruit
Depati	Rimba	position in Orang Rimba with duty to lead the court and administer justice
duku	Indonesian	type of langsat fruit
dukun	Rimba	shaman, practitioner of traditional medicine
dunia	Indonesian	world, earth
durian	Indonesian	large Southeast Asian fruit with a characteristic odor and a spiky husk
dusun	Indonesian	village
E		
Eda	Batak	title for *Batak* women meaning sister
G		
gank	Rimba	gang or group of people
gelogoh	Rimba	pieces of wood used to make floors in a house
genah	Rimba	hamlet of 3 to 10 huts
guntor	Rimba	local fruit shaped like an olive but purple like grape
H		
hopi, hopi beik	Rimba	no, no good or out of place
hukum sio-sio	Indonesian	bad karma
I		

Ibu	Indonesian	mother, also used as term of respect, ma'am
Ibu guru	Indonesian	female teacher
Ibu mantri	Indonesian	female nurse
Indok	Rimba	mother
induk rapah	Rimba	queen bee

J

Jenang	Rimba	person outside the jungle that function as mediator, advisor and trusted intermediary when Orang Rimba sell forest products
jerenang	Rimba	rattan, the rattan sap is taken from the fruit, known as dragon's blood, and receives a high price

K

kabupaten	Indonesian	regency or district, an administrative subdivision of a province in Indonesia
kafir	Arabic	person who rejects Islam, a non-believer
kail	Indonesian	hook, used by Butet to describe the letter J
kemang	Rimba	type of mango
kerakai	Indonesian	branch, used by Butet to describe the letter K
kertas	Indonesian	Paper

ketoprak	Indonesian	typical Javanese street food with rice steamed in a banana leaf, tofu, sliced cabbage, bean sprouts and rice crackers with a peanut sauce
koin	Rimba	length of traditional cloth, similar to Indonesian *kain*
kubu	Malay	exonym ascribed to nomadic animist people living in the rainforests of Southeast Sumatra. This is a derogatory term to describe Orang Rimba connoting primitive, wild, dirty, and unintelligent.
kujur	Rimba	spear
L		
lantak	Rimba	wooden climbing pegs
lima	Indonesian	five
M		
malam	Indonesian	evening
mandiri	Indonesian	independent
Mangku	Rimba	position within the Orang Rimba with duties similar to a member of parliament; community spokesman
mbak	Javanese	title for Indonesian women, primarily on Java, meaning sister

melangun	Rimba	when a group of Orang Rimba moves away from an area when one of their members dies. Death is a sign of great misfortune and so, to forget the sadness more quickly, the group must move on.
melawon	Indonesian	cool (attitude, style)
Melayu	Indonesian	Malay
Menti	Rimba	position within the Orang Rimba with communication officer duties; he makes invitations, passes messages, information and news to the whole community, negotiates and mediates
mercon	Rimba	matchstick placed under a nail that you thump hard using a piece of wood to make an explosion, a firecracker
muntaber	Indonesian	gastroenteritis, general illness with vomiting and diarrhea

N

nangoy	Rimba	white pig, different from *bebi*, a black pig or boar
Nano-nano	Indonesian	Indonesian candy with three flavors: sweet, sour, and salty
napol	Rimba	grey, clay-like riverbed

O

ojek	Indonesian	motorcycle taxi, passenger rides behind driver
Orang Luar	Rimba	description used by Orang Rimba to describe the non-rainforest dwellers, "people outside"
Orang Rimba	Rimba	description used by the people of the rainforest in Jambi Province to describe themselves to outsiders, possibly in use for a number of generations
Orang Terang	Rimba	description used by Orang Rimba to describe the non-rainforest dwellers, "people in the light"

P

Pak	Indonesian	father, from *Bapak*, also used as term of respect, sir or mister
pantun	Indonesian	traditional form of poetry, a four-line verse with a fixed rhythm and rhyme scheme
paracetamol		over-the-counter pain reliever and fever-reducer
peci	Rimba	cap shaped like a truncated cone and usually made from black velvet or cotton
pemungkuy	Rimba	bundle of one hundred sarongs, weighing approximately 30-40 kilograms
pena	Indonesian	pen

pencak silat	Indonesian	Indonesian martial art focused on training for self-defense
pesaken	Rimba	household or nuclear family
piagam	Rimba	charter
pisang	Rimba	Type of hardwood used by Orang Rimba to make *lantak*, not to be confused with Indonesian word for banana
putus	Rimba	"quit", used by Orang Rimba to say "has completed school"
puwor	Rimba	type of fruit tree, *kecombrang* in Indonesian

R

rambut	Indonesian	Hair
rambutan	Indonesian	tropical fruit with red skin covered with thin, pliable spines that give it a "hairy" appearance
rapah	Rimba	bee, bee larva
Rimba	Rimba	jungle, rainforest, the dialect spoken by Orang Rimba
rombong	Rimba	a group of Orang Rimba
rumbai	Rimba	type of leaves used to weave mats
rupiah	Indonesian	official currency of Indonesia, in 1999 US$1 = IDR 15,000, in late 2011 US$1 = IDR 9,000

rusa	Indonesian	deer

S

selembedo	Rimba	venomous ants
selese	Rimba	"finish", used by Orang Rimba to say "has dropped out of school"
seluang	Rimba	type of leaf used to make storage bags especially for tobacco or rice
setali bukit	Indonesian	range of hills
sialang	Rimba	very tall tree (perhaps more than 200 feet tall) where beehives are located, means "beehive" in Indonesian
simpur miyang	Rimba	type of rattan vine, strong enough to be used as rope
sokola	Rimba	School
SP A, SP B	Indonesian	Settlement Unit A, B; abbreviation for Satuan Pemukiman A, B
sudung, sudung pesaken	Rimba	hut, family hut
sungai	Indonesian	river
susudungon	Rimba	temporary hut, the suffix—on can be used to mean little or toy. The huts used by the school where often not well built.

T

tampoy	Rimba	type of fruit similar to mangosteen

tana peranaon	Rimba	site set aside for women nearing/during childbirth
tano	Rimba	area of 100 square meters
Temenggung	Rimba	Orang Rimba chief
tempe	Indonesian	fermented soya bean cake (delicious!)
Tengganai	Rimba	advisor to the *Temunggung* (chief)
topi	Indonesian	hat
Transmigra-tion unit		settlement consisting of around 300 households
tuju gembung	Rimba	Hexes
tunom	Rimba	type of tree bark that burns like a sparkler to chase the bees away while harvesting honey

U

undang nan delapan	Rimba	"The eight laws", Orang Rimba traditional law, consisting of *empat di pucuk* (four above) and *empat di bewoh* (four below)

W

Waduh!	Indonesian	an exclamation, like gee!
Wakil	Rimba	Deputy

Y

Yoya	Rimba	"That is . . ."

Other Notes

Fido Dido

cartoon character created by Joanna Ferrone and Susan Rose and used on merchandise around the world to spread the message "be relaxed with who you are"

Malin Kundang

Indonesian folktale about a mother's retribution exacted from her ungrateful son

SOKOLA

A non-profit organization that delivers of educational programs for indigenous people living in the Jambi rainforest and other remote areas in Indonesia

Thomson and Thompson

the incompetent twin detectives in *The Adventures of Tintin*, the series of classic Belgian comic books written and illustrated by Hergé

WARSI

Indonesian NGO community conservation network

Reading Group Questions and Discussion Topics for *The Jungle School*

1. Part I of *The Jungle School* retains the form of the author's journals as she wrote them while in the jungle. How does the journal format help the reader to really understand what the author is thinking and feeling? How does this format cloud the reader's perception of life in the jungle?

2. The author's goal is to bring education to the Orang Rimba, the People of the Rainforest. Yet, in Chapter 3, the Orang Rimba accuse Butet of meddling with their traditions by trying to teach their children. Do you think that the Orang Rimba need education? How will literacy affect their traditions?

3. One of the author's reasons for educating the Orang Rimba is so that they can safeguard the rainforest. Are the Orang Rimba adequately prepared to face the challenges of protecting the rainforest? Compare how the Orang Rimba treat the rainforest versus how the Orang Terang use this land.

4. As a woman working and traveling alone within a community where women stay with their families, the author is often subject to questions. How does Butet deal with the gender issues she faces? What do you think of the Orang Rimba's approach to women and the role women play in their society? How does the role of Rimba women differ from your expectations?

5. The author is a trained anthropologist, yet her approach with the Orang Rimba is not anthropological. Do you think Butet's involvement with the children is a better approach than the observer role she attributes to anthropologists? What are the benefits and shortcomings of her friendly approach?

6. Several times, the author refers to events that do not have a rational explanation—her feeling at the honey tree in Chapter 1, Diki's anti-bee-sting ring in Chapter 2, the fear of hexes among the Forestry Department officials in Chapter 2. What role does the supernatural play in the lives of the Orang Rimba? How might their beliefs be used in the preservation of the rainforest?

About the Author

Butet Manurung was born in Jakarta, Indonesia in 1972. She developed a love of the outdoors while earning her degrees in anthropology and Indonesian literature from Padjajaran University, Bandung, Indonesia. In 1999, Butet joined the conservation NGO, WARSI, to lead their educational program for the Orang Rimba, the "people of the forest" indigenous to the rainforests of Jambi. Her work in the jungle evolved into co-founding SOKOLA, a non-profit providing educational opportunities for marginalized people in remote areas throughout Indonesia.

As an educator and activist, she has received international recognition—UNESCO's "Man and Biosphere Award" in 2001, TIME Magazine's "Hero of Asia" in 2004, Ashoka Fellowship in 2006, "Asia Young Leader" in 2007 and World Economic Forum "Young Global Leader" in 2009. *The Jungle School* is her first book, originally published in Indonesian as *Sokola Rimba* in 2007.

About SOKOLA

Established in 2003 by Butet Manurung and four fellow educators, SOKOLA provides educational opportunities for indigenous peoples in remote areas of Indonesia. SOKOLA uses a practical "reading-writing-counting" method developed during Butet's years living among the Orang Rimba in the jungles of Jambi. The mission of this non-profit organization is to prepare isolated communities to deal with the challenges of the ever-encroaching modern world.

As of today, SOKOLA has reached a dozen communities across Indonesia, bringing literacy to more than 10,000 individuals, both children and adults.

For more information about SOKOLA, please visit our website at *www.sokola.org* or e-mail us at *rumasokola@yahoo.com*.

Proceeds from this publication support SOKOLA.

CPSIA information can be obtained
at www.ICGtesting.com
Printed in the USA
LVHW03s1717180618
581091LV00002B/551/P